ESTHE

THE EXILEE

WHO

BECAME QUEEN

ESTHER

THE EXILEE

WHO

BECAME QUEEN

THE INSTITUTION OF PURIM

DR. JEAN NORBERT AUGUSTIN

(BMM, MMM, DMM, DD, Th.D)

COPYRIGHT

NORBOOKS
The Word Became Flesh

ACKNOWLEDGMENTS

All my gratitude to the Holy Spirit for His unfailing guidance without which the writing of this book would not have been possible.

My heartfelt thanks to Mr. Michael Johnson, Chief Editor of the WEB (World English Bible) from which all quoted Scriptures – except otherwise stated – have been taken.

EPIGRAPH

"Then Mordecai bade them return answer to Esther, Don't think to yourself that you shall escape in the king's house, more than all the Jews.

For if you altogether hold your peace at this time, then will relief and deliverance arise to the Jews from another place, but you and your father's house will perish: and who knows whether you haven't come to the kingdom for such a time as this?" (Esther 4:13-14).

Table of Contents

PREFACE

Of the sixty-six books in the Bible, only two are named after women: ESTHER and RUTH.

A formidable feature of ESTHER is that not once is God mentioned in this book! Yet, the Bible is supposed to be all about Him!

Does that mean that God is entirely absent in this book?

Not at all!

On the contrary, ESTHER shows us how, from "backstage", the Almighty works wonderfully through people and circumstances! Though not explicitly mentioned, He is no less present, as we shall see.

In DANIEL, the Babylonian king, Nebuchadnezzar, had a very strange dream which not one of his astrologers and diviners could interpret.

Daniel and his three close companions – Meshach, Shadrach and Abednego – were then in captivity in Babylon along with other Jews.

The dream was about a gigantic and bizarre statue made of various elements: gold, silver, brass, iron and clay.

Thanks to wisdom given to him by God, Daniel proposed to interpret the king's dream, thereby saving the lives of the astrologers and diviners whom the king had threatened to put to death.

In his interpretation, Daniel told the king that the statue represented a number of kingdoms that would succeed one another in the course of time.

The statue's head of gold, Daniel explained, represented the kingdom of Babylon under Nebuchadnezzar. Indeed, Babylon, in those days, was the richest, the strongest and the most glorious kingdom on earth. Of the seven wonders of the ancient world, one was Babylonian: the much celebrated hanging gardens!

Daniel went on to explain the king's dream, saying that the second part of the statue was going to be a less glorious kingdom that would supplant Babylon.[1]

Indeed, as time passed, Babylon was conquered by Persia in alliance with Media.

Thus, the new world power became Medo-Persia.

It's worth noting that Persia has now become Iran, the archenemy of Israel!

The other kingdoms that would follow were Greece under Alexander the Great, the Roman Empire and eventually Christ's Earthly Kingdom that will, one day, destroy and supplant all earthly kingdoms.

---

[1] Daniel 2:31-45.

For a detailed study of Nebuchadnezzar's dream and its interpretation, see my series *"Revelation Revisited"*.[2]

When Persia defeated Babylon, king Cyrus the Great allowed the Jewish captives to return to their land. However, some chose to remain in Persia – among them, Esther.

Herein lies the first intervention of God!

Indeed, we may ask why would Esther want to remain in a foreign land where she was living in exile while the king, himself, had given the exilees permission to return to their homeland?

Absurd!

---

[2] Dr. Jean Norbert Augustin: *"Revelation Revisited –* Volumes 1-7.

Or, was it God's plan?

As the story unfolds, we shall see more clearly whether it was foolishness on the part of Esther or whether there was some sound reason for her choice of remaining in her captor's country.

The story of Esther covers the period extending approximately from 479 BC to 473 BC.[3]

The place is Shushan, the capital of the Persian Empire.

But who was that Esther?

---

[3] Crosswalk.com: Britt Mooney: "5 Reasons All Christians Should Read Queen Esther's Story", updated June 25, 2021. Accessed 26 June 2024.

She was a Jewess, daughter of Abihail. Orphaned, she was raised by Mordecai, her father's nephew. As we said above, both had remained in Persia in spite of king Cyrus's authorization to return to Jerusalem.

Her Hebrew name was Hadassah, which means "myrtle". Later on, she was given the Persian name "Esther" which means "star".

Do we know who wrote ESTHER?

The author has not been precisely identified. But three names are commonly associated with the book: Ezra, Nehemiah and Mordecai, Esther's elder cousin.

The book ESTHER is particularly important to the Jews because, in it, lies the origin of the great Jewish festival called *"Purim"* which has become one of the most important festivals of the Jewish calendar.

As we study the story of Esther, we shall discover the flow of events that led to the coming into existence of this wonderful festival.

More of that in the final chapter of the book.

For the time being, let's go directly to the book.

CHAPTER 1

THE SETTING

"Now it happened in the days of Ahasuerus (this is Ahasuerus who reigned from India even to Ethiopia, over one hundred twenty-seven provinces),

that in those days, when the king Ahasuerus sat on the throne of his kingdom, which was in Shushan the palace,

in the third year of his reign, he made a feast to all his princes and his servants; the power of Persia and Media, the nobles and princes of the provinces, being before him;

when he shown the riches of his glorious kingdom and the honor of his excellent majesty many days, even one hundred eighty days.

When these days were fulfilled, the king made a feast to all the people who were present in Shushan the palace, both great and small, seven days, in the court of the garden of the king's palace.

[There were hangings of] white [cloth], [of] green, and [of] blue, fastened with cords of fine linen and purple to silver rings and pillars of marble: the couches were of gold and silver, on a pavement of red, and white, and yellow, and black marble.

They gave them drink in vessels of gold (the vessels being diverse one from another), and royal wine in abundance, according to the bounty of the king.

The drinking was according to the law; none could compel: for so the king had appointed to all the officers of his house, that they should do according to every man's pleasure."[4]

T he story of Esther can, in some measure, be compared to a classical tragedy like those of the Greco-Roman period or of seventeenth century Europe.

---

[4] Esther 1:1-8.

However, a classical tragedy comprises five Acts. But, ESTHER is an extended tragedy made up of more than double the number of Acts – so numerous and so dramatic are the turns of events!

Just like ancient tragedies, ESTHER is set in the confine of a king's palace. In Rome, that would be in the palace of an Emperor, rather. With all the characters being present, friction is bound to brood, instigated by love, passion, jealousy, envy, ambition, political interest and nepotism.

Typically, the story begins on a low key. The main characters are introduced – either by their physical presence on the stage or by reference to them.

However, in spite of the light atmosphere prevailing, the germ of the tragedy is also present - lurking backstage, as it were, eagerly waiting for the *Fatum's*[5] call to get into action.

Let's get into the story and see how all this plays out.

FEAST NO. 1

---

[5] Fatum: Latin word meaning "what has been spoken". Word that has given birth to the word "Fate". Merriam-Webster Dictionary, Accessed 23 July 2024.

The story takes place in king Ahasuerus's palace in Shushan, the capital of the Persian Empire. Ahasuerus's other name was Xerxes. He reigned over an extremely vast Empire extending from India to Ethiopia and covering one hundred and twenty-seven provinces.

We already get an idea of Ahasuerus's wealth and power.

During the third year of his reign, the king gave a party in honour of the princes, his servants, the nobles and all the high personalities of all his provinces.

During the feast, the king exhibited his extravagant wealth, luxury and the sumptuousness of his kingdom.

That feast lasted … one hundred and eighty days – full six months or half a year!

To help keep track of the story, I'll call this feast "Feast No. 1". Indeed, one characteristic of the Book of Esther is the impressive number of feasts held by the king and the queen.

FEAST NO. 2

Once the above-mentioned feast was over, the king gave another feast for his subjects living in Shushan, the capital. His feast was held in the palace's garden, delicately and sumptuously decorated. There were multi-coloured hangings in white, green and blue fastened to silver rings and to the marble pillars with cords of fine linen and purple.

Purple, as we know, is the colour of royalty. In the Gospel, Jesus tells the story of a very rich and selfish man who was dressed in purple and who feasted every day. At his door, lay a famished beggar who craved the little bits and pieces of bread that fell from the rich man's table. But the latter never once deigned to throw a piece of bread to the beggar.

One day, they both died. The once miserable beggar was taken by angels to Abraham's Bosom – a periphrase for Paradise - while the heartless rich man found himself burning in an eternal fire.[6]

I'm not going to comment further on this anecdote, my main purpose being to underscore the value of purple.

Luke, the author of the Book of Acts, also mentions a rich lady, called Lydia, who dealt in purple. Paul and his companions met her in

---

[6] Luke 16:19-31.

Philippi at a prayer meeting by a riverside. The lady believed and was baptized along with her household. Then she invited Paul and his companions to lodge at her place.[7]

It is also a well-known fact that, at royal functions and high profile ecclesiastical ceremonies, purple is very much present as the preferred colour!

Going back to king Ahasuerus's feast, one can imagine all the pageantry exhibited in that immense marquee! The pavement was of red, white, green and black marble. On it, were set couches of gold and silver.

---

[7] Acts 16:13-15.

Wine was lavishly served in vessels of gold – each of a different type. However, following the king's explicit command, wine was to be served only to those who wanted it. It wasn't to be forced upon anybody.

As the kingdom covered a vast number of provinces – one hundred and twenty-seven – the king must have been sensitive to his guests' personal taste and culture.

The extravagance of that feast, to a certain degree, reminds us of the fastuous reception king Solomon gave to the Queen of Sheba during her visit to the king![8]

As king Ahasuerus's feast was open to all his subjects who lived in Shushan – irrespective of class – one may wonder whether nobody was tempted to leave the party with one of those gold wine vessels hidden under their clothes! In our day and age, chances are a number of those gold vessels would have "walked away" from the feast to enrich a few!

As we have seen, the story begins in a very festive atmosphere. We see an extravagantly wealthy monarch with a populistic penchant. Something else that's evident is his self-conceit as in his craving to exhibit his opulence to his guests.

Last but not least, we have been introduced to an important element – wine!

Indeed, at the table of ancient oriental kings and Roman Emperors, wine was always lavishly served.

The stress I'm placing on wine is far from being unwarranted. Wine will, indeed, play an important role in the story. It will, in fact, be the element that will trigger tragedy.

CHAPTER 2

QUEEN VASHTI IS BANISHED

In certain orthodox Oriental cultures, it is customary for the society to be sexually segregated. Men and women do not usually mix at certain functions like weddings.

I live in Mauritius which has a multiracial and multicultural population. And I've spent most of my teaching career in environments highly populated with Hindus and Muslims. So, I know what I'm saying.

We are going to see this in play in the story of Esther.

FEAST NO. 3

"Also Vashti the queen made a feast for the women in the royal house which belonged to king Ahasuerus.

On the seventh day, when the heart of the king was merry with wine, he commanded Mehuman, Biztha, Harbona, Bigtha, and Abagtha, Zethar, and Carcass, the seven chamberlains who ministered in the presence of Ahasuerus the king, to bring Vashti the queen before the king with the crown royal, to show the peoples and the princes her beauty; for she was beautiful to look on.

But the queen Vashti refused to come at the king's commandment by the chamberlains: therefore was the king very angry, and his anger burned in him"[9].

Indeed, while king Ahasuerus was entertaining his guests in his palace garden, his wife, Queen Vashti, was holding another feast in the royal house. This feast was exclusively reserved for women.

---

[9] Esther 1:9-12.

Although the Bible does not give further details about this feast, we may easily guess it was no less luxurious than the two "male" feasts the king had organized. Indeed, the female guests must have been the wives and daughters of the king's male guests.

No wonder, the women were dressed in their best Oriental outfits, wore their costliest jewellery and had their faces delicately made-up. The air in the king's house must have been filled with the choicest Oriental perfume!

TROUBLE STARTS

On the seventh day – the last day of Feast No. 2 - king Ahasuerus was inebriated. During all the days the two feasts had lasted, he must have had his fill of wine!

He ordered his seven chamberlains - Mehuman, Biztha, Harbona, Bigtha, and Abagtha, Zethar, and Carcass to fetch Queen Vashti with her royal crown on her head. His aim was to show his guests how beautiful a woman the Queen was.

But, quite unexpectedly, the Queen refused to accede to the king's request!

That was the spark that triggered the fire!

THE KING SEEKS COUNSEL

"Then the king said to the wise men, who knew the times, (for so was the king's manner toward all who knew law and judgment;
and the next to him were Carshena, Shethar, Admatha, Tarshish, Meres, Marsena, and Memucan, the seven princes of Persia and Media, who saw the king's face, and sat first in the kingdom),
What shall we do to the queen Vashti according to law, because she has not done the bidding of the king Ahasuerus by the chamberlains?
Memucan answered before the king and the princes, Vashti the queen has not done wrong to the king only, but also to all the princes, and to all the peoples who are in all the provinces of the king Ahasuerus.

For this deed of the queen will come abroad to all women, to make their husbands contemptible in their eyes, when it shall be reported, The king Ahasuerus commanded Vashti the queen to be brought in before him, but she didn't come.

This day will the princesses of Persia and Media who have heard of the deed of the queen say [the like] to all the king's princes. So [will there arise] much contempt and wrath.

If it please the king, let there go forth a royal commandment from him, and let it be written among the laws of the Persians and the Medes, that it not be altered, that Vashti come no more before king Ahasuerus; and let the king give her royal estate to another who is better than she.[10]

In a fit of anger, the king sought counsel with seven high dignitaries who were well versed in Persian law. They were Carshena, Shethar, Admatha, Tarshish, Meres, Marsena, and Memucan – seven of Medo-Persian princes who sat constantly in the king's presence and who were next to the king in importance.

The king asked those eminent personalities what sanction – according to the law of the land – should be taken against the Queen for having refused to obey his command.

---

[10] Esther 1:13-19.

Memucan – one of the seven advisers – told the king that the Queen's disobedience was an offense directed not only to the king, but to all the men of the kingdom! Soon, the news of the Queen's disobedience would spread all across the one hundred and twenty-seven provinces of the kingdom. Following the queen's bad example, all the women of the kingdom would disobey their husbands and refuse to submit to their authority. The princes of Persia and Media also would follow Queen Vashti's example and, thus, all the princes would be dishonoured.

QUEEN VASHTI IS SANCTIONED

When the king's decree which he shall make shall be published throughout all his kingdom (for it is great), all the wives will give to their husbands honor, both to great and small.

The saying pleased the king and the princes; and the king did according to the word of Memucan:

for he sent letters into all the king's provinces, into every province according to the writing of it, and to every people after their language, that every man should bear rule in his own house, and should speak according to the language of his people."[11]

---

[11] Esther 1:13-22.

Memucan went further in his condemnation of the Queen. He suggested that the king issue an irrevocable decree banning the Queen from the king's presence for ever and that her royal position be given to a better woman than she.

That decree, Memucan advised, should be published all over the kingdom so that women everywhere would take cognizance of it and give to their husbands the submission, the allegiance and the respect due to them.

Memucan's advice so pleased the king that he followed it to last letter. He wrote the decree, had it translated into every language spoken in all the provinces of the kingdom so that it would be understood by one and all.

Furthermore, the decree stipulated that every man should exercise his authority over his household and speak the language of his own people.

End of Act I.

CHAPTER 3

ANALYSING THE PROBLEM

Having seen how the trouble started, we may ask ourselves a few questions.

The first one should address the root of the problem.

Was Queen Vashti right or wrong in refusing to respond to the king's request to appear before him?

The answer would have to be yes and no.

She was wrong because, in those days, the society was patriarchal – that is, governed by men. This was even more so in Oriental cultures.

In refusing to attend to Ahasuerus's request, she was committing an act of insubordination towards her husband. That was a serious offense if we realize that, even in the New Testament, women are commanded to submit to their husbands' authority:

"Wives, be subject to your own husbands, as to the Lord.

For the husband is the head of the wife, and Christ also is the head of the assembly, being himself the savior of the body."[12]

Secondly, Vashti's act of rebellion was not only directed towards her husband: more seriously, she was committing an offense towards her *king*! Indeed, not only was Ahasuerus her *husband* – he was her *king,* too! Her rebellion was tantamount to a crime of *"lèse majesté"* - a crime (such as high treason) committed against a sovereign power, an offence violating the dignity of a ruler as the representative of a sovereign

---

[12] Ephesians 5:22-23.

power".[13] Her refusal to do the king's bidding was an even greater affront as it happened in the presence of the king's guests!

Thirdly, in the context of a patriarchal society, as a woman, she was supposed to respect a man – in this case, Ahasuerus.

In short, Vashti's disobedience was towards her husband, towards her king and towards a man – Ahasuerus being all three.

Fourthly, she was wrong in *not* giving a reason for her refusal. She *may* have given an excuse. But, based on the Bible narrative, we don't see any justification that she gave.

---

[13] "Lèse-majesté." Merriam-Webster.com Dictionary, Merriam-Webster, https://www.merriam-webster.com/dictionary/l%C3%A8se-majest%C3%A9. Accessed 28 Jun. 2024.

Let's now try to find some justification for Vashti's disobedience.

She may have disobeyed because the order was transmitted to her by chamberlains – her subordinates. Maybe she considered it an offence before her guests to be ordered by the royal court's employees. Had the king come in person – or sent some higher court's officer - her response might have been different!

A better justification she may have had is the fact that her husband wanted to parade her in front of his guests as if she was a mere object!

Indeed, we are told in the narrative that the king was exhibiting all his luxurious possessions before the eyes of his guests. In his state of drunkenness, he may have committed the folly of considering his wife as just another one of his "collectibles"!

In short, the Queen may have felt debased, humiliated!

Another "attenuating circumstance" Queen Vashti may have had was the fact that she would be exhibited before a host of drunken men. Not only was that debasing, but one never knows to what extremes men filled with wine could have gone with a beautiful woman like Vashti! Especially as her husband was a weak king who gave far too much leeway to his counsellors as is demonstrated by what was to follow.

For king Ahasuerus and his counsellors, Esther was viewed as a rebel. But, modern day feminists will, no doubt, consider her as a heroine – a pioneer and a precursor of the "Women's Lib Movement"!

But, let's not forget that, no matter what was going on in Ahasuerus's palace and no matter how we, human beings, view the situation, God – though not named – was in full control and was seeing to it that things went *His* way!

CHAPTER 4

IN SEARCH OF A NEW QUEEN

Now that Vashti had lost king Ahasuerus's favour and had been banished, a new queen had to be found.

Let's see how the king was going to proceed.

After these things, when the wrath of king Ahasuerus was pacified, he remembered Vashti, and what she had done, and what was decreed against her.

Then said the king's servants who ministered to him, Let there be beautiful young virgins sought for the king:

and let the king appoint officers in all the provinces of his kingdom, that they may gather together all the beautiful young virgins to Shushan the palace, to the house of the women, to the custody of Hegai the king's chamberlain, keeper of the women; and let their things for purification be given them;

and let the maiden who pleases the king be queen instead of Vashti. The thing pleased the king; and he did so." [14]

---

[14] Esther 2:1-4.

In the aftermath of the stormy events that had happened at the king's court, the king must have spent his time feasting and carousing to forget his wayward wife.

Once the feast was over and he regained his sobriety, the thought of Vashti's rebellion and banishment came back to him.

ENTER THE KING'S COUNSELLORS

Those in Ahasuerus's service came forward with a proposal. They suggested that the king send officers to all the provinces of the kingdom. Their mission? Search for all the most beautiful virgins and bring them to the royal compound. There, they were to be lodged in the "women's house", under the care of one Hegai, the king's chamberlain. Hegai was to give the maidens assembled all the creams, lotions, powders and perfumes that were required for their purification and beautification.

PREPARATION OF THE PROSPECTS

That period of preparation was essential and lasted one full year! It was a determining factor because the maidens would have to go by turns to the king's personal chamber: the one who would please him the most would be crowned queen!

This gives an idea of the romantic and the matrimonial culture of the Persian culture of that time. We see how oriental monarchs placed a premium on feminine beauty and attractiveness! King Ahasuerus's sexual behaviour is not different from that of king Solomon's. The *"Song of Solomon"* in the Bible amply bears testimony to this. And this penchant for eroticism has lingered to this day in oriental regions.

What we saw in the previous chapter and what we see now tell us also how ancient kings liked to surround themselves with a host of counsellors. Those were highly influential – even in very intimate matters like the choice of a wife. We can better assess their influence when we realize that, in advising the king about the choice of a wife, they were also determining who would be their queen!

No wonder the suggestion put forward by the king's servants pleased him. Accordingly, he went forward with the plan with the aim of finding himself a new wife.

ENTER ESTHER AND MORDECAI

"There was a certain Jew in Shushan the palace, whose name was Mordecai, the son of Jair, the son of Shimei, the son of Kish, a Benjamite,

who had been carried away from Jerusalem with the captives who had been carried away with Jeconiah king of Judah, whom Nebuchadnezzar the king of Babylon had carried away.

He brought up Hadassah, who is, Esther, his uncle's daughter: for she had neither father nor mother, and the maiden was fair and beautiful; and when her father and mother were dead, Mordecai took her for his own daughter." [15]

We are now going to be introduced to two new characters who will play key roles in this this drama.

---

[15] Esther 2:5-7.

When king Nebuchadnezzar took the Jews into captivity in Babylon, there was, among the exiles, a man called Mordecai. He was the son of one Jair, a distant relative of Saul, Israel's first king.

Along with him was a young girl called Hadassah. She had been an orphan since childhood. Mordecai, her elder cousin, had consequently adopted her and raised her. When eventually the Medo-Persians conquered Babylon, Mordecai and Hadassah were taken to Shushan, the capital of the Persian Empire.

For some unknown reason, when the Persian king, Cyrus, allowed the Jewish captives to return to Jerusalem, Mordecai and Hadassah chose to remain in Shushan.

I say for "some unknown" reason because, at that time, nobody – not even the two persons concerned – knew why they had decided to remain in the Persian capital!

But the events that would follow will show that there was a very good reason for that apparently absurd decision!

However, the wise and prudent Mordecai had instructed his young protégée not to divulge her nationality nor the relationship between them.

Faithful in his responsibility as Esther's guardian, Mordecai everyday remained in the vicinity of the king's court – more precisely close to the women's house. He daily enquired about his protégée to know how she was faring.

Meanwhile, her Jewish name had been changed to Esther, a Persian name. The myrtle – the meaning of Hadassah - had turned into a star – the meaning of Esther!

End of Act 2.

CHAPTER 5

THE PLAN IS PUT INTO ACTION

"So it happened, when the king's commandment and his decree was heard, and when many maidens were gathered together to Shushan the palace, to the custody of Hegai, that Esther was taken into the king's house, to the custody of Hegai, keeper of the women.

The maiden pleased him, and she obtained kindness of him; and he speedily gave her things for her purification, with her portions, and the seven maidens who were meet to be given her out of the king's house: and he removed her and her maidens to the best place of the house of the women.

Esther had not made known her people nor her relatives; for Mordecai had charged her that she should not make it known.

Mordecai walked every day before the court of the women's house, to know how Esther did, and what would become of her."[16]

W hen the king's decree was executed and his officers fine-combed the kingdom in search

---

[16] Esther 2:8-11.

of the most beautiful virgins for the king, Hadassah found herself among those chosen. Indeed, she was a virgin and of a very great beauty, too.

She was, therefore, taken to King Ahasuerus's palace compound and kept in the women's house along with all the other virgins who had been identified by the king's officers.

For greater clarity, I'm now going to refer to the young maiden as Esther and not Hadassah.

In the king's house, Esther found favour from Hegai, the king's eunuch in charge of the female prospects. Hegai gave her whatever she needed for her purification and beauty care. Besides, she was well fed and was even given seven maids to attend to her. Best of all, she and her seven maids were moved to different quarters – to the choicest section of the women's house!

Let's now see now how the chosen virgins were to behave from then on.

"Now when the turn of every maiden was come to go in to king Ahasuerus, after it had been done to her as prescribed for the women twelve months (for so were the days of their purification accomplished, [to wit], six months with oil of myrrh, and six months with sweet odors and with the things for the purifying of the women),

then in this wise came the maiden to the king: whatever she desired was given her to go with her out of the house of the women to the king's house.

In the evening she went, and on the next day she returned into the second house of the women, to the custody of Shaashgaz, the king's chamberlain, who kept the concubines: she came in to the king no more, except the king delighted in her, and she were called by name." [17]

As we said above, the young girls' preparation lasted one full year. During the first six months, they were given oil and

---

[17] Esther 2:12-14.

myrrh for their purification and, during the next six months, they had perfumes of sweet odours to further beautify them and make them desirable.

After that, they were called, one of them each night, to pass from the women's house to the king's private room. On leaving the women's house, they were free to take with them whatever they wanted.

After they had spent the night with the king, on the next day they were sent to another section of the palace's compounds reserved for the king's concubines. There, they were placed under the care of another eunuch called Shaashgaz.

From then on, they could not appear before the king in his private quarters unless he had been fully satisfied with them. In such cases, he would call those "lucky" ones by name. It was only on these conditions that a concubine could reappear before the king!

Thus we see how oriental kings had a lustful life. No doubt that must have aroused a lot of jealousy and animosity among the chosen maidens. The competition must have been very ferocious for the king's favour and rise to the rank of queen!

ESTHER'S TURN TO GO TO THE KING

"Now when the turn of Esther, the daughter of Abihail the uncle of Mordecai, who had taken her for his daughter, was come to go in to the king, she required nothing but what Hegai the king's chamberlain, the keeper of the women, appointed. Esther obtained favor in the sight of all those who looked at her.

_So Esther was taken to king Ahasuerus into his house royal in the tenth month, which is the month Tebeth, in the seventh year of his reign.

The king loved Esther above all the women, and she obtained favor and kindness in his sight more than all the virgins; so that he set *the royal crown on her head, and made her queen instead of Vashti.*"[18]

Now came Esther's turn to spend the night with the king. When she left the women's house, she was entitled to whatever she desired to take with her. However, she took nothing apart from what Hegai, the chamberlain, gave her.

Not only did she find favour with Hegai, but everybody who saw her loved her!

When she was introduced into the king's private room and she spent the night with him, she so pleased him that she found the

---

[18] Esther 2:15-17.

king's favour, too. The monarch lavishly bestowed all kinds of kindness upon her.

King Ahasuerus was so pleased with Esther – much more than with any of the other maidens – that he put the royal crown upon her head.

Thus, Esther became queen in the place of the banished Vashti.

FEAST NO. 4

"Then the king made a great feast to all his princes and his servants, even Esther's feast; and he made a release to the provinces, and

gave gifts, according to the bounty of the king.

When the virgins were gathered together the second time, then Mordecai was sitting in the king's gate.

Esther had not yet made known her relatives nor her people; as Mordecai had charged her: for Esther did the commandment of Mordecai, like as when she was brought up with him."[19]

As we have already said, the Book of Esther is full of feasts. King Ahasuerus was such a pleasure loving monarch!

---

[19] Esther 2:18-20.

To celebrate the accession of Esther to the royal throne, the king organized a feast in her honour. To that feast were invited all the princes of the kingdom and all those in the king's service.

On that occasion, there were great joy and celebrations in all the kingdom and gifts were generously given according to the riches of the king.

As Esther had been instructed by his cousin Mordecai not to reveal their relationship nor the family to which she belonged, we don't know whether Mordecai was invited to the feast.

However, Mordecai was more concerned with something else: his protégée's welfare.

So he was constantly seen sitting within the palace's gate.

Little did he know that his unflinching assiduity would serve a grand purpose!

End of Act 3.

CHAPTER 6

MORDECAI SAVES THE KING'S LIFE

"In those days, while Mordecai was sitting in the king's gate, two of the king's chamberlains, Bigthan and Teresh, of those who kept the threshold, were angry, and sought to lay hands on the king Ahasuerus.

The thing became known to Mordecai, who shown it to Esther the queen; and Esther told the king [of it] in Mordecai's name.

When inquisition was made of the matter, and it was found to be so, they were both hanged on a tree: and it was written in the book of the chronicles before the king."[20]

One day, as Mordecai was sitting at the palace's gate, according to his custom, he overheard a conversation between two of the king's chamberlains, Bigthan and Teresh. For some unknown reason, the two men were boiling with anger against the king.

Was it because they had been severely reprimanded by the king for some failure in their duty? Or was it because they had not

---

received a favour or a promotion they had been expecting?

The narrative does not mention the reason for their anger.

But it must have been very great for the two men were plotting against the king's life!

Fortunately, Mordecai was there and happened to be privy to the conversation!

Conscientiously, he had the message sent to Esther, the queen, through contacts who had access to her.

Quite naturally, she promptly and dutifully informed the king, her husband, about the plot and the plotters. In so doing, she mentioned the name of Mordecai as the informer – in twenty-first vocabulary, the whistle blower!

The king took the matter very seriously. He had an inquiry made into the matter and found that it was ... founded!

Accordingly, the two plotters were unceremoniously hanged on a tree!

The matter was of such paramount importance that it was recorded in the book of chronicles in the personal presence of the king.

The circumstances that would follow would demonstrate the importance of Mordecai's role in the plot against the king's life.

Indeed, little did Mordecai and Esther know how the information they exchanged would change their lot and that of their countrymen completely! It would even bear consequences lasting to this day!

End of Act 4.

CHAPTER 7

RELECTIONS ON THE EVENTS

L et us now pause the story and try to reflect upon what we have seen so far.

We said, in thc preface, that one peculiarity of the book of Esther is that God is never mentioned in this book. Although He is known by a number of names, not one of them is mentioned in ESTHER!

But, as we also said in the preface, this does not mean that He is *not* really present! On the contrary, He is very much present and active in the story!

Let's see how.

To begin with, how can we explain that Mordecai and Esther chose to remain in Persia while they had been given full authorization to return to their homeland? Would they not have been much safer among their close ones and their relatives? Did they not fear lest another less indulgent king came to the throne of Persia and started persecuting them? Even if they felt a sense of security, did they not fear another invader captured them and took them into exile somewhere else as had been the case with the Babylonians?

What kept them in Persia – or rather, Who?

Secondly, the trouble started with Vashti's refusal to obey the king's command which, itself, was motivated by the fact that the king was inebriated. But why did he have to drink that much to commit such a folly as request his wife to come and parade herself before drunken guests?

Far from me to imply that it was God who made the king drink himself out of his wits! But what I'm saying is why did Ahasuerus have to drink that much to lose all his common sense?

Thirdly, Vashti was a happy and wealthy queen. She was married to the world's most powerful monarch of the day. While the king was carousing with his male guests, she was free to throw her own party for her female guests – and, all that, with the king's bountiful resources. Why did she have to object to the king's order? Did she not know that the society then was patriarchal and that women had to submit to their husbands? Did she not know that her disobedience would be an affront to the king in front of his guests? Was she not aware that her rebellion might bring about regrettable consequences?

How can the queen's senseless decision be explained?

Fourthly, following Vashti's defiance of the king's command, why did the king have to consult counsellors to enquire of them what should be done to his wife? How can we explain that the king of the most powerful kingdom on earth was so weak as to rely on his subordinates' advice? Did the king not know that his issue with his wife was … dirty linen and that dirty linen is not supposed to be washed in public?

Fifthly, the king's counsellors were, no doubt, ambitious people craving the king's favour and quick to do anything to please him in order to achieve their aim. Their "verdict" against the queen was unquestionably a harsh one. But, what from the vantage point of Esther? Was it not a boon for her - for Vashti's misfortune turned to her advantage?

Sixthly, Esther was only a poor captive girl taken into captivity to Babylon then to

Shushan. Now she was, as it were, "lost" somewhere in the vast Persian Empire.

There surely were many very beautiful girls in all of the one hundred and twenty-seven provinces of the kingdom. What was the probability of Esther, that poor orphaned captive, finding herself among the chosen maidens?

Seventhly, what explains that Esther found such immediate favour from Hegai who was in charge of the maidens that she received a special treatment – to the extent of being moved to special quarters along with her maids?

Eighthly, when it was her turn to go to the spend the night with the king, what special treatment did she give the king that she pleased him more than all the other virgins? Was she the last of all the chosen maidens to go to the king's private room? Else, how could the king compare her performance with that of all the others? Otherwise, how could the king know those coming after her wouldn't outdo her performance? Being given the number of maidens standing in line to go to the king, the probability that she was the very last one is very flimsy!

Ninthly, with regard to the murder plot, how come that Mordecai overheard the plotters' conversation? Granted he was constantly near the palace's gate. But were Bigthan and Teresh so foolish as to discuss a plan of *that* magnitude without making sure there was nobody within hearing distance? Were they *that* indiscreet?

Tenthly, was it sheer coincidence that that event was registered in the book of chronicles in the very presence of the king?

Eleventhly, what or Who, one night, caused the king to be sleepless?

Twelfthly, why did the king, that night, desire that, of all books, the book of chronicles be read to him?

These apparent "details" were to be of the utmost importance as the story unfolded.

The points discussed above are just a few reflections that we can make when we ponder the events that have taken place so far in ESTHER.

After much thought, we are bound to conclude that, behind the scene, there must have been an Invisible Hand guiding the

characters and the circumstances. Also, behind that Invisible Hand, there must have been a Superior Intelligence at work!

To every effect there is a cause. Consequently, if there was a Superior Intelligence directing the events from behind the scene, there must have been a very good reason for that!

As we proceed with the study of Esther, we shall discover the noble cause behind everything that happens in the story.

In ESTHER, there are so many "coincidences" that they must all form part of a plan – and a Divine one at that!

CHAPTER 8

ENTERS THE VILLAIN

At the beginning of chapter 1, I said that the story of Esther can be compared to a classical tragedy.

So far, we have seen the main male character – King Ahasuerus – the main female character – Queen Esther – and the trouble that has begun to brood with Vashti's rebellion and the hanging of two plotters.

We still need to see one key character step onto the scene: the villain!

This is what we are going to see now.

"*After these things did king Ahasuerus promote Haman the son of Hammedatha the Agagite, and advanced him, and set his seat above all the princes who were with him.*

All the king's servants, who were in the king's gate, bowed down, and did reverence to Haman; for the king had so commanded concerning him. But Mordecai didn't bow down, nor did him reverence.

Then the king's servants, who were in the king's gate, said to Mordecai, Why disobey you the king's commandment?

Now it came to pass, when they spoke daily to him, and he didn't listen to them, that they told Haman, to see whether Mordecai's matters would stand: for he had told those who he was a Jew."[21]

For some unnamed reason, king Ahasuerus elevated a certain Haman to power. That man was the son of one Hammedatha, an Agagite. He was also a descendant of Amalek, a sworn enemy of Israel.[22]

The king raised Haman above all the other princes and commanded that people should bow down to him to pay him homage.

---

[21] Ester 3:1-4.
[22] Exodus 17:14-16.

Mordecai, however, refused to bow down to him. As a good Jew, he would bow to nobody but to God. Similarly, Daniel and his three Hebrew companions refused to bow down and worship be it king Nebuchadnezzar or the gigantic statue he built![23]

Those near the palace's gate noticed that Mordecai did not bow to Haman. They questioned him about his refusal and he revealed to them his Jewish appurtenance.

In spite of their repeated questionings, Mordecai remained firm and adamant!

---

[23] Daniel 3:12-30. Daniel 6:1-28.

Finally, they reported the matter to Haman and that wicked man began to concoct a devilish plan to avenge himself.

"When Haman saw that Mordecai didn't bow down, nor did him reverence, then was Haman full of wrath.

But he thought scorn to lay hands on Mordecai alone; for they had made known to him the people of Mordecai: therefore Haman sought to destroy all the Jews who were throughout the whole kingdom of Ahasuerus, even the people of Mordecai.

In the first month, which is the month Nisan, in the twelfth year of king Ahasuerus, they cast Pur, that is, the lot, before Haman from day to day, and from month to month, [to] the twelfth [month], which is the month Adar."[24]

Wounded in his ego and fuming with a devilish anger, Haman devised a sadistic plan. Having learned that Mordecai was a Jew, he planned to destroy not only the offender but his whole people that was in Ahasuerus's kingdom!

From the first month, Nisan, to the twelfth month, Adar, they cast lots – called *Pur* – before Haman to decide upon a date for the execution of Haman's heinous plan.

---

[24] Esther 3:5-7.

"Haman said to king Ahasuerus, There is a certain people scattered abroad and dispersed among the peoples in all the provinces of your kingdom; and their laws are diverse from [those of] every people; neither keep they the king's laws: therefore it is not for the king's profit to allow them.

If it please the king, let it be written that they be destroyed: and I will pay ten thousand talents of silver into the hands of those who have the charge of the [king's] business, to bring it into the king's treasuries". [25]

Haman informed the king that there was, scattered in his kingdom, a people with

---

[25] Esther 3:8-9.

strange laws. They neither conformed to the kingdom's laws nor obeyed the king's orders. Hence, it was not profitable for the king to keep that people in the kingdom.

Haman went as far as offering to finance the genocidal project to the tune of ten thousand talents of silver talents. Undoubtedly, that must have represented a formidable sum! He would hand the money over to the person who would carry out the project and that person, in turn, would pour it into the king's coffers.

The idea so pleased the king that he took his signet ring and gave it to Haman.

"The king took his ring from his hand, and gave it to Haman the son of Hammedatha the Agagite, the Jews' enemy. The king said to Haman, "The silver is given to you, the people also, to do with them as it seems good to you."

Then the king's scribes were called in on the first month, on the thirteenth day of the month; and all that Haman commanded was written to the king's local governors, and to the governors who were over every province, and to the princes of every people, to every province according to its writing, and to every people in their language. It was written in the name of King Ahasuerus, and it was sealed with the king's ring."[26]

By giving his signet ring to Haman, the king was, in fact, surrendering to him all his authority. The king's signet ring was very precious insofar as it was used to put the royal seal to any document, law, edict or decree emanating from the king.

Provided with the king's signet ring, Haman, that evil man, had *"carte blanche"*[27]. Thus, he could act as he willed. He was virtually the king!

---

[26] Esther 3: 10-12.
[27] Full discretionary power.

The king's madness went to the extent that he authorized Haman to keep the ten thousand silver talents and use it any way he willed. He further surrendered the Jews to Haman's whims and mercy.

You bet that evil man didn't dilly-dally. He summoned all the kingdom's scribes and dictated to them, in the name of the king, the terms of his genocidal plan against the Jews. When, at the end of the decree, he put the royal seal to it with the king's signet ring, he, at the same time, sealed the Jews' lot!

Copies of the decree were made in the various languages spoken in the one hundred and twenty-seven provinces of the kingdom so that it would be intelligible to everybody.

Those copies were then dispatched by couriers to every prince and governor of the kingdom so that, on the appointed day, the plan would be put into execution – no pun meant!

"Letters were sent by couriers into all the king's provinces, to destroy, to kill, and to cause to perish, all Jews, both young and old, little children and women, in one day, even on the thirteenth day of the twelfth month, which is the month Adar, and to plunder their possessions. A copy of the letter, that the decree should be given out in every province, was published to all the peoples, that they should be ready against that day. The

couriers went out in haste by the king's commandment, and the decree was given out in the citadel of Susa. The king and Haman sat down to drink; but the city of Susa was perplexed."[28]

Notice how radical the massacre of the Jews was to be: destroy, kill, cause to perish, plunder! And not one was to be spared: men, women, children, the young, the elderly would all have to fall victim to Haman's hatred!

---

[28] Esther 3:13-15.

Accordingly, couriers rushed to every one of the provinces to take copies of the decree to the respective princes and governors.

When the decree went out and the Jews took cognizance of it, panic – quite understandably - seized them! We can imagine how their fright and their anguish went crescendo as months and days went by, drawing closer the day appointed for the massacre!

Satisfied with themselves and with their Machiavellian plan, the king and Haman sat down to drink!

End of Act 5.

CHAPTER 9

TAKING STOCK OF THE SITUATION

With the arrival of Haman on the scene and his phenomenal elevation to power, the drama gains in intensity.

Indeed, in the story of Esther, this man represents the devil, himself. The devil, as we know, has always hated the Jews because they are God's chosen people.

In the Old Testament, we remember how, in Egypt, the Pharaoh – another instrument in the hands of the devil – ordered the massacre of all male newborns. He even ordered the two Hebrew midwives, Shiphrah and Pua, to abort male babies even while the women were in labour.[29] However, fearing God, the two midwives allowed the male babies to be born, thus causing the Pharaoh's anger. Thereafter, he ordered the taskmasters to make the Hebrew slaves' work much harder.

Baby Moses miraculously escaped that massacre and was, later on, sent back to Egypt to set the Hebrews free.[30]

---

[29] Exodus 1:15.
[30] Exodus 3.

During the third and second centuries BC, Antiochus IV Epiphanes[31] – a type of the antichrist - also carried out a brutal persecution against the Jews, which led to the rebellion of the Maccabees.[32]

In 70 AD, the Roman General Titus[33] invaded Jerusalem with his ruthless army. They conquered Jerusalem and destroyed the Second Temple. Following that, the surviving Jews fled Jerusalem and were scattered everywhere.

---

[31] Wikipedia: Antiochus IV Epiphanes: king of the Seleucid Empire (215 BC – 164 BC). Accessed 08 July 2024.
[32] Ibid.
[33] Wikipedia: "Titus": Titus Caesar Vespasianus (30 Dec 39 AD – 13 Set 81 AD). Accessed 08 July 2024.

A last example we are going to cite is king Herod's massacre of male babies in the hope of killing the newborn Jesus in the process.[34]

The most notorious case in modern times is, without contest, the *Holocaust* commanded by the German Fuhrer, Adolf Hitler. That genocidal project was known as "the Final Solution to the Jewish Question" and was … executed – no pun meant - by Adolf Eichmann.[35]

During the *Holocaust*, more than six million Jews were massacred in the concentration camps. There was no lack of means for the Nazis to bring their plan to fruition: gas,

---

[34] Matthew 2.
[35] https://www.britannica.com/biography/Adolf-Eichmann. Accessed 08 July 2024.

electricity, gun shots, lethal injections, crematory chambers and so on. The end truly justified the means!

During my high school days, I once read a book about that terrible period. In it, were pictures of belts, bags, lampshades and other objects made of – believe it – Jews' skins!

The reason I've been mentioning these examples of Jewish persecutions and massacres is to place the plan concocted by Haman in its broadest context possible.

Indeed, there has always been a devilish plan to destroy Israel because the Israelites are God's chosen people ever since He made a covenant with Abram – later to become Abraham:

"Now Yahweh said to Abram, "Leave your country, and your relatives, and your father's house, and go to the land that I will show you. I will make of you a great nation. I will bless you and make your name great. You will be a blessing. I will bless those who bless you, and I will curse him who treats you with contempt. All the families of the earth will be blessed through you."[36]

"Yahweh appeared to Abram and said, "I will give this land to your offspring."[37]

Even in our modern times, there are countries and nations that have vowed to utterly

---

[36] Genesis 12:1-3.
[37] Genesis 12:7.

annihilate the Israelites and blot Israel from the face of the globe!

Except that these nations don't know what the Bible says their end will be:

"This will be the plague with which Yahweh will strike all the peoples who have fought against Jerusalem: their flesh will consume away while they stand on their feet, and their eyes will consume away in their sockets, and their tongue will consume away in their mouth"![38]

Haman, therefore, was yet another instrument in the hands of the devil. His mission was to

---

[38] Zechariah 14:12.

accomplish the devil's top priority wish: destroy God's people!

His plan was concocted against the backdrop of a universal and sempiternal master plan to destroy the Israelites.

We have seen how the plan he concocted was evil, sadistic and methodical. He cunningly managed to secure the king's approval and even offered a huge sum of money to see his plan come to fruition.

Lots – *Pur* – were cast to decide upon a date for the massacre to take place. The decree was to be written in all the languages spoken in all the kingdom's provinces for everybody to clearly understand what it was all about.

All that was devised in such a way as to put the Jews in a sadistic anguish!

Just imagine the plight in which Haman's decree had put the Jews! They had been given authorization to return to their homeland but had chosen to remain behind. Now, away from their country and their loved ones, Damocles's[39] sword was hanging over their heads!

Who would be able to save them from such a dire situation? Was there somebody able to rescue them? If there was some help available, whence would it come?

---

[39] Wikipedia: Damocles: a courtier in the court of Dionysius I of Sicily.
Accessed 15 July 2025.

But, let's not forget, Israel is God's people! Although not explicitly named, He was there, watching over His people! And now, He decided to set things in motion so as to save His people as He had always done.

CHAPTER 10

MORDECAI PERSUADES ESTHER

"Now when Mordecai found out all that was done, Mordecai tore his clothes and put on sackcloth with ashes, and went out into the middle of the city, and wailed loudly and bitterly. He came even before the king's gate, for no one is allowed inside the king's gate clothed with sackcloth. In every province, wherever the king's commandment and his decree came, there was great mourning among the Jews, and fasting, and weeping, and wailing; and many lay in sackcloth and ashes."[40]

---

[40] Esther 4:1-3.

Mordecai, as we've already said, was to play a key role in the story. When he learned about the detestable decree, he went into a fast. As was the custom of the day, he tore his clothes put on a sackcloth and threw ashes upon his head. He went everywhere, weeping, wailing and lamenting over his compatriots' fate. In so doing, he was showing empathy towards his fellow countrymen. Indeed, throughout the kingdom, the people were in a desperate situation.

As no-one was allowed into the king's court, Mordecai came as close as he could to the palace's gate. He longed to send news to Esther about the situation outside. As queen, she might do something to come to the rescue of the Jews, her own poor and miserable countrymen.

"Esther's maidens and her eunuchs came and told her this, and the queen was exceedingly grieved. She sent clothing to Mordecai, to replace his sackcloth, but he didn't receive it. Then Esther called for Hathach, one of the king's eunuchs, whom he had appointed to attend her, and commanded him to go to Mordecai, to find out what this was, and why it was."[41]

Having seen in what miserable attire Mordecai was clothed, Esther's servants and her eunuchs went to report the matter to the queen. Quite naturally, she was utterly

---

[41] Esther 4:4-5.

grieved to learn in what state her faithful and devoted guardian was. She, therefore, commanded Hathach, one of her personal eunuchs, to go and enquire of Mordecai the reason of his mourning.

"So Hathach went out to Mordecai, to the city square which was before the king's gate. Mordecai told him of all that had happened to him, and the exact sum of the money that Haman had promised to pay to the king's treasuries for the destruction of the Jews. He also gave him the copy of the writing of the decree that was given out in Susa to destroy them, to show it to Esther, and to declare it to her, and to urge her to go in to the king to

make supplication to him, and to make request before him for her people."[42]

Hathach at once executed the queen's order. Mordecai informed him of the dire situation in which the Jews found themselves. He especially mentioned the phenomenal sum of money Haman had offered to the king in return of the pleasure of exterminating the Jews. To confirm what he was saying, Mordecai also handed over to Hathach a copy of the decree to be given to the queen. Finally,

---

[42] Esther 4:6-8.

Mordecai requested that Esther go to the king and plead in favour of the Jews.

"Hathach came and told Esther the words of Mordecai. Then Esther spoke to Hathach, and gave him a message to Mordecai: "All the king's servants and the people of the king's provinces know that whoever, whether man or woman, comes to the king into the inner court without being called, there is one law for him, that he be put to death, except those to whom the king might hold out the golden scepter, that he may live. I have not

been called to come in to the king these thirty days."[43]

When Hathach reported to the queen what Mordecai had said and handed her a copy of the decree, she sent the eunuch back to Mordecai with a message from her.

She informed her cousin that there was, in the country, a very strict law. It stipulated that whoever – man or woman – entered the king's presence without having been called should be put to death.

---

[43] Esther 4:9-11.

Only if the king held out his royal scepter towards that person would he or she be spared.

The problem was that Esther had not been called by the king the last thirty days! She might never be called again and, hence, never be able to appear before him!

At that stage, it looked like the situation had reached a deadlock. The plight of the Jews was without issue. A real *cul de sac* – a blind alley!

Damocles's sword was about to fall right upon them!

Inexorably!

Where was God? Would He allow His children to undergo such a massacre? Would the wicked and hateful Haman have his way? Would he be allowed to prevail?

When the Israelites were in servitude in Egypt and they cried out to God, He heard them and He sent Moses to rescue them from Egyptian bondage.

Would He hear this time? If He does, who would He send to save His children from Haman's folly? Would there be another Moses?

"They told Esther's words to Mordecai. Then Mordecai asked them to return this answer to

Esther: "Don't think to yourself that you will escape in the king's house any more than all the Jews. For if you remain silent now, then relief and deliverance will come to the Jews from another place, but you and your father's house will perish. Who knows if you haven't come to the kingdom for such a time as this?"[44]

The intermediaries went to report Esther's words to Mordecai. But the latter – out of love, concern and compassion for his countrymen - wouldn't settle for that! Spurred by a profound sense of patriotism, he sent a very severe message to his young

---

[44] Esther 4:12-14.

cousin. He asked the mediators to tell Esther not to think that, if she kept quiet, she alone, of all Jews, would be spared once the massacre got underway. She and all her household would perish likewise.

Then Mordecai added two threatening warnings: Let not Esther think that if she kept quiet, help wouldn't come: help would come from elsewhere!

Secondly, the wise and thoughtful Mordecai tactfully told the mediators to ask Esther why she, an exile, had been elevated to the rank of queen. Was it not for such a time as that?

"Then Esther asked them to answer Mordecai, "Go, gather together all the Jews

who are present in Susa, and fast for me, and neither eat nor drink three days, night or day. I and my maidens will also fast the same way. Then I will go in to the king, which is against the law; and if I perish, I perish." So Mordecai went his way, and did according to all that Esther had commanded him."[45]

You bet, Mordecai's terse words cut Esther to the quick! They had hit the bull's eye! She must, indeed, have been shocked by the unusually severe tone of his otherwise affectionate and protective guardian's message. Wounded in her royal ego, she must have realized that it was vanity on her part to

---

[45] Esther 4:15-17.

think that, apart from her, no-one could intervene in favour of the Jews.

Reference to the danger facing herself and her family must have shaken her, too. She might have thought that, because of her royal position, she would be spared. But Mordecai's words must have brought her down from her throne and back to reality.

But what, of everything that Mordecai told her, must have had the greatest effect upon her is, I'm convinced, the reason why she had come to the throne!

Indeed, who would have thought that Hadassah, an orphaned Jewish girl in exile would, one day, become queen Esther in the very country where she was in exile?

When she pondered her elder cousin's words, the young woman must have realized there, indeed, *must* have been a purpose behind her election as queen! As the wise Mordecai had told her, it *must* have been for a time like *that*!

Getting out of her apathy, Esther sent word to Mordecai to assemble all the Jews in Susa (Shushan) and ask them to observe a three-day full fast – eating and drinking nothing. She and the maidens in her service would do likewise.

What she was going to say next was massive! It was going to be the pivot – the turning point of the story! Those words of hers needed to be carved in stone.

After the three-day fast, she would defy the king's order and enter his private chamber – called or not called!

"And if I perish, I perish!" she adamantly resolved.

Strengthened by the queen's determination, Mordecai promptly went about gathering all the Jews in Susa to publicize the three-day fast she had commanded.

End of Act 6.

CHAPTER 11

MORDECAI'S KEY ROLE

Mordecai is unquestionably one of the most important characters in ESTHER – if not the most important!

He was Esther's elder cousin. As Esther was an orphan – having neither father nor mother – Mordecai took her under his care and brought her up.

When the Jews were captured by the Babylonians and taken into exile, Mordecai faithfully stayed close to her young protégée.

Later, when the Persians defeated Babylon, the Jewish exilees were moved to Shushan, the capital of the Persian Empire. Still, the two cousins kept together.

The good King Cyrus allowed the Jews to return to Jerusalem. But, for some reason, the two chose to remain in Persia. As Esther was but a young girl, I suspect it must have been the older, the wiser and the more perspicacious Mordecai who took that decision.

Had he been divinely instructed to do so?

Another person in his place would have chosen to return to Jerusalem where he would have been safer and where the "burden" of keeping watch over her young cousin would have been greatly lessened – if not lifted - in the midst of their close ones.

Mordecai could, thus, have found himself a life partner, settled down and founded a family.

But the man was a responsible person. He was, no doubt, sensitive to God's prompting and leading. He must have subconsciously known that his presence and that of his young cousin would, one day, be needed in Persia.

The events that followed proved him right for, had the pair left Persia, Esther would never have been queen in that country!

Would that have allowed Haman's evil plan to go ahead unhindered?

One may argue that Haman's anger was ignited because of Mordecai's refusal to bow to him and that with Mordecai gone back to Jerusalem, there would have been no reason for that detestable man's anger to burst as it did.

But the devil is so mad against God's people – and he's always been - that he would have found some other means to try to put his plan into action.

Mordecai's devotion to Esther is seen in the fact that, even after she has been crowned queen, he is constantly seen near the palace's gate. His main concern is for his protégée's welfare. He is always enquiring of the palace's personnel about Esther.

Again, now that her young cousin has been established queen of Persia, is his duty not over? Has she not obtained all the favour and security one can dream of? Can Mordecai not start thinking about his own life and his own happiness?

Yet, he chooses to continue watching over Esther.

It's thanks to his assiduity in the vicinity of the palace that he happens to overhear the two traitors plotting against the king's life.

That is a very important moment in the story. That's another major turning point in this tragedy!

Indeed, it's thanks to his denunciation of the plotters that his name is recorded in the chronicles.

Later on, it's his recognition by the king that triggers Haman's downfall and, eventually, his death by execution.

From then on, Mordecai becomes the king's favourite. He is lifted above all the princes and high dignitaries of the kingdom.

Thanks to his newly acquired position, he takes matters in his hands, revokes Haman's decree, saves the Jews from destruction and turns a banished and condemned people into a people to be feared!

Mordecai's role in this story is not only beautiful, but one with consequences lasting to this day!

CHAPTER 12

ESTHER'S SECRET SCHEMING

With the king's approval of Haman's genocidal scheme and the issuance of the decree, the tragedy had reached its culminating point. The Jews' lot had been sealed. It was only a question of time before Persian swords would be drawn and Jewish blood flow in the streets of Susa and of all the other provinces! Soon, the kingdom would be filled with cries, screams and groanings as Jewish blood would gush out of gurgling throats.

But where was God? Would He keep silent and let Haman have his way? Would He allow His children to be exterminated while He sat quietly on His Throne? Would He lend a deaf ear to His children's cries?

Far from it!

God the Almighty hears when His children call upon Him, especially in times of great need.

"This poor man cried, and Yahweh heard him, And saved him out of all his troubles"[46].

"For the eyes of the Lord are on the righteous, And his ears open to their prayer;

---

[46] Psalm 34:6.

But the face of the Lord is against those who do evil".[47]

The exchange of messages between Mordecai and Esther culminates in the turning point in this tragedy. The real pivot, however, is Esther's resolution to enter the prohibited quarters even if she's not called, thus transgressing the king's order. But the most determining factor remains her magnanimous declaration: "If I perish, I perish!"

---

[47] 1 Peter 3:12.

"Now it happened on the third day, that Esther put on her royal clothing, and stood in the inner court of the king's house, over against the king's house: and the king sat on his royal throne in the royal house, over against the entrance of the house.

It was so, when the king saw Esther the queen standing in the court, that she obtained favor in his sight; and the king held out to Esther the golden scepter that was in his hand. So Esther drew near, and touched the top of the scepter.

Then said the king to her, What will you, queen Esther? and what is your request? it shall be given you even to the half of the kingdom."[48]

After the three-day fast was over, Esther put on her royal garments and ventured into the king's personal quarters. From where the king sat on his throne, he had a full view of Esther drawing near.

The tension must have risen sky high! What would the king's reaction be? Remember how Vashti had been repudiated for having dared disobey Ahasuerus's command! Would Esther not suffer the same lot – especially as the king was in the habit of consulting his evil and favour-seeking

---

[48] Esther 5:1-3.

advisers - even with regard to matrimonial affairs - and blindly acting upon their interest-motivated advice?

Would the ambitious Haman not gladly welcome an opportunity to climb a little higher in the king's esteem if only he could do the king some service by blaming Esther for her audacity?

Nevertheless, undaunted, Esther kept on advancing towards the king. Miraculously, the king held out his scepter and Esther touched it. That signified that the king consented to welcome her.

Then he asked Esther what her request was. He went even further: even if it was half of his kingdom that she wanted, he'd be prepared to give it to her!

It's strange how "easy" it was for ancient kings to give away half of their kingdoms!

We remember also how, later on, king Herod would be prepared to offer half of his kingdom to Herodias's daughter, Salome, just for a dance! But against all odds,

prompted by her mother, Salome asked for the head of John the Baptist![49]

We have seen how vast Ahasuerus's kingdom was: it extended from India to

---

[49] Mark 6:21-29.

Ethiopia. Imagine what half of such an empire represented!

But that did not interest Esther. She had quite a different plan!

*"Esther said, If it seem good to the king, let the king and Haman come this day to the banquet that I have prepared for **him.***

Then the king said, Cause Haman to make haste, that it may be done as Esther has said. So the king and Haman came to the banquet that Esther had prepared."[50]

[50] Esther 5:4-5, emphasis added.

Instead, she invited the king to a banquet – Feast No. 5 - that she had prepared for him but requested that Haman come along, too. And the king granted her request.

In view of the urgency of the situation, one may say what a bizarre request to make to the king! Bizarre and absurd when we realize that Esther might have obtained half of Ahasuerus's kingdom!

Imagine an orphaned and exiled young Jewish maiden becoming queen over a kingdom half the size of Ahasuerus's!

Moreover, was it not insane to hold a banquet after a three-day fast?

Was it not an ill-chosen time to hold a banquet when all the Jews were weeping, crying, wailing and lamenting?

And what an absurd request that Haman – the abominable enemy of the Jews – should be invited to that banquet?

"For my thoughts are not your thoughts, neither are your ways my ways, says Yahweh.

For as the heavens are higher than the earth, so are my ways higher than your ways, and my thoughts than your thoughts."[51]

---

[51] Isaiah 55:8-9.

Indeed, God works in mysterious ways. Although not "personally and physically" present, He was, nevertheless, maneuvering backstage! He was in full control of the situation!

You bet Haman gladly and proudly accepted the invitation! What a privilege for him to be invited by the queen to a banquet organized in honour of the king! He was thus climbing yet another rung up the social ladder! It was, as it were, yet another medal pinned to his breast!

*"The king said to Esther at the **banquet of wine**, What is your petition? and it shall be granted you: and what is your request? even*

to the half of the kingdom it shall be performed.

Then answered Esther, and said, My petition and my request is:

if I have found favor in the sight of the king, and if it please the king to grant my petition, and to perform my request, let the king and Haman come to the banquet that I shall prepare for **them**, and I will do tomorrow as the king has said.

Then went Haman forth that day joyful and glad of heart: but when Haman saw Mordecai in the king's gate, that he didn't *stand up nor move for him, he was filled with wrath against Mordecaï*"[52].

At the banquet, wine was, as usual, served in profusion. Again, king Ahasuerus asked queen Esther what her request was. He reiterated his offer of half of his kingdom should the queen desire it.

But that was not what Esther wanted: she was concealing her secret plan under her hat – sorry her crown!

Quite surprisingly – not to say irrationally – she asked the king to come to *yet* another banquet – Feast No. 6 - that she was going to

---

[52] Esther 5:6-9, emphasis added.

organize in honour of *both, himself and Haman*!

We may wonder what was going on in the queen's head. What was the point in holding a banquet to which she invited the king and Haman so as to invite them to yet another banquet to be held … on the next day?

Notice that the previous banquet was in honour of the king. Now, the next banquet was to be in honour of both men, Ahasuerus and Haman!

This seemingly nonsensical series of banquets and invitations baffles our understanding even more when we remember that the queen had just ended a three-day fast and, worse still, that her countrymen were in a most dire situation! And, to add insult to injury, the wicked and ruthless Haman – the mastermind behind the genocidal scheme – was then sitting at the queen's table and was even going to be guest of honour at the forthcoming banquet!

All that arouses our curiosity as to what Esther was secretly planning. Let's move on to discover what it was all about.

End of Act 7.

CHAPTER 13

THE COUNSELLOR COUNSELLED

"Then went Haman forth that day joyful and glad of heart: but when Haman saw Mordecai in the king's gate, that he didn't stand up nor move for him, he was filled with wrath against Mordecai.

Nevertheless, Haman refrained himself, and went home; and he sent and fetched his friends and Zeresh his wife.

Haman recounted to them the glory of his riches, and the multitude of his children, and all the things in which the king had promoted him, and how he had advanced him above the princes and servants of the king.

Haman said moreover, Yes, Esther the queen did let no man come in with the king to the banquet that she had prepared but myself; and tomorrow also am I invited by her together with the king.

Yet all this avails me nothing, so long as I see Mordecai the Jew sitting at the king's gate."[53]

O n the next day, proudly and joyfully, Haman went to the banquet. However, when he

---

[53] Esther 5:9-13.

arrived at the palace's gate, there stood, according to his custom, his hated enemy, Mordecai!

Contemptuously, Mordecai didn't stand up nor made a move for him – and, even less, bowed to him!

That hurt the villain in his ego. Mordecai was a real thorn in his flesh! He was filled with anger, but chose to gulp down his ego. He would wait to give Mordecai the mule's kick.[54] For him, vengeance was a dish that's best eaten cold!

---

[54] Alphonse Daudet (13 May 1840 – 16 December 1897). Story of a Pope's mule that waited seven years to take its revenge over a naughty kid by giving him a fatal kick.

When he was back home, he assembled his wife Zeresh and his friends and boasted to them about the high honour to which the king had elevated him – even above princes. He told them how privileged he was to have been the sole guest at the king's banquet and added that, on the following day, he was again going to be the sole guest with the king at the queen's banquet. And he bragged about the phenomenal wealth he had accumulated.

However, all that meant nothing to him for there was something that marred his happiness: the sight of Mordecai, the Jew, standing at the palace's gate and obstinately refusing to budge for him! That made his blood boil in his veins!

"Then said Zeresh his wife and all his friends to him, Let a gallows be made fifty cubits high, and in the morning speak you to the king that Mordecai may be hanged thereon: then go you in merrily with the king to the banquet. The thing pleased Haman; and he caused the gallows to be made".[55]

Hearing that, his wife and his friends gave him an advice. They asked him to have a gallows made – fifty cubits high.[56] In the morning, he should speak to the king to tell him that Mordecai should be hanged on it. Once Mordecai was dead, he would be able to confidently and joyfully go to the banquet.

---

[55] Esther 5:14.

[56] Google: Unit Converter: About twenty-three metres or seventy-five feet.

The idea greatly pleased Haman and he ordered a gallows to be made.

Again we see how King Ahasuerus and Queen Esther were fond of holding banquets. This, however, was not a feature limited to them or to Persian monarchs. We remember how King Solomon of Israel also held magnificent banquets – for example, during Queen Sheba's visit.[57] During the era of the Roman Empire, kings and emperors, too, organized feasts that often ended in orgies.

During such feasts, wine was served in profusion and, in their drunkenness, very often awful things happened. There is, for

---

[57] 1 Kings 10.

example, the beheading of John the Baptist during King Herod's birthday party.[58]

Similarly, in the book of Esther, we see how banquets were legion and how wine was at the source of many problems.

Another feature of royal courts of those days was the habit that monarchs had of keeping favourites and counsellors around them. Those favourites and counsellors were, most of the time, ambitious people seeking their self-interest. In order to achieve and maintain this, they were prepared to do anything.

What, very often, played to their advantage was the monarchs' weakness and reliance on

---

[58] Matthew 14:6-12.

their counsellors for advice. And, most of the time, the advice was ill-inspired.

We have seen how king Ahasuerus sought advice from his counsellors with regard to the treatment to be administered to Vashti for her non-compliance with the king's order. The advice given was that Vashti should be banished and a new queen chosen.

It's true that, from God's vantage point, the advice went in the proper direction. But, on the human plane, was it ethical for a king to ask advice from his subordinates to tackle a domestic problem? Was it proper for a monarch of Ahasuerus's caliber and repute to - as it were - wash the royal couple's dirty linen in public?

We have seen how Haman's advice to the king with regard to the Jews gave birth to the hateful decree!

And now, we have just seen what advice Zeresh and Haman's friends have given to the king's main adviser.

Will their advice work to Haman's good?

This is what we shall see in the next chapter.

End of Act 8.

CHAPTER 14

HAMAN'S HUMILIATION

As we have already said, though not explicitly mentioned in ESTHER, God is, nevertheless, very present in this story. From behind the curtain – like a film director - He directs and is in control of all the events taking place.

His children, the Jews, were in danger of being massacred. Was He going to intervene in the situation? If so, how was He going to come to His children's rescue?

On that night the king couldn't sleep; and he commanded to bring the book of records of the chronicles, and they were read before the king.

It was found written that Mordecai had told of Bigthana and Teresh, two of the king's chamberlains, of those who kept the threshold, who had sought to lay hands on the king Ahasuerus.

The king said, What honor and dignity has been bestowed on Mordecai for this? Then the king's servants who ministered to him said, "Nothing has been done for him."[59]

---

[59] Esther 6:1-3.

God works in mysterious ways[60] and speaks in various ways.[61] That night, the king couldn't sleep. His insomnia, however, had a purpose: God willed it!

This reminds us that Pilate's wife also couldn't sleep the night her husband was judging Jesus. She was being so tormented in her sleep that she sent a message to her husband, warning him not to have anything to do with Jesus for He was a righteous Man.[62]

To while away the time, the king asked that the Book of Records be brought and be read to him.

---

[60] Psalm 34:6.
[61] Hebrews 1:1.
[62] Matthew 27:19.

The Book of Records was a kind of diary which chronicled all the important events taking place in the kingdom.

What a bizarre request that was! Imagine we can't find our sleep and, in the middle of the night, we ask that the telephone directory be brought and be read to us! What a strange way that would be to lull us to sleep!

When the Book of Records was read to the king, the reader came to the place where was mentioned the plot concocted by Bigthana and Teresh – plot that was thwarted by Mordecai's denunciation.

Remembering how his life had been spared thanks to Mordecai, the king asked whether he had been rewarded for his good service. Quite incredibly, the answer was "No"!

"The king said, "Who is in the court?" Now Haman was come into the outward court of the king's house, to speak to the king to hang Mordecai on the gallows that he had prepared for him.

The king's servants said to him, Behold, Haman stands in the court. The king said, Let him come in." [63]

Thereupon, the king noticed somebody in the courtyard and asked who it was. When told

---

[63] Esther 6:4-5.

that it was Haman, the king asked that he be shown in.

The king's insomnia must have lasted the whole night and the reading of the Book of Records must have gone on till the early hours of the morning for Haman was supposed to go and see the king in the morning to have Mordecai hanged.

"So Haman came in. The king said to him, What shall be done to the man whom the king delights to honor? Now Haman said in his heart, To whom would the king delight to do honor more than to myself?

Haman said to the king, For the man whom the king delights to honor, let royal clothing be brought which the king uses to wear, and the horse that the king rides on, and on the head of which a crown royal is set:

and let the clothing and the horse be delivered to the hand of one of the king's most noble princes, that they may array the man therewith whom the king delights to honor, and cause him to ride on horseback through the street of the city, and proclaim before him, Thus shall it be done to the man whom the king delights to honor."[64]

As we said above, the king was in the habit of consulting his chamberlains and counsellors on certain matters.

---

[64] Esther 6:6-9.

He, therefore, asked for a piece of advice from Haman. But it was a most bizarre and unexpected one. He asked Haman what he should do to a man whom he, the king, wished to honour.

At once, Haman's thoughts rushed to himself! Who else but him could the king wish to honour? Had he not already had ample proof that the king wanted him to ascend above all the other high dignitaries of the kingdom?

The egoistic and egocentric Haman told the king that the man whom His Majesty wished to honour should be dressed in the king's royal garments and be given the king's personal horse wearing a royal crown.

Endowed with an insatiable ambition, he asked that the king give instructions to one of the most prestigious princes to take the royal garments and dress him therewith and place the crown on the horse's head, himself.

As if that was not enough, he asked that that prince parade that man on horseback across the city of Shushan, shouting:

"This is what the king does to the man whom it pleases him to honour!"

In spite of His reverence, God sometimes has a great sense of humour as we are going to see.

"Then the king said to Haman, Make haste, and take the clothing and the horse, as you have said, and do even so to Mordecai the Jew, who sits at the king's gate: let nothing fail of all that you have spoken.

Then took Haman the clothing and the horse, and arrayed Mordecai, and caused him to ride through the street of the city, and proclaimed before him, Thus shall it be done to the man whom the king delights to honor."[65]

To Haman's utter discomfiture, the king commanded him to personally take the royal clothing, the horse and the crown. Then the king commanded him to dress Mordecai and

---

[65] Esther 6 :10-11.

set the crown on the horse's head. And, for his greatest humiliation, the king ordered him to parade Mordecai on horseback across the city, shouting: "This is what the king does to the man whom it pleases him to honour!"

What a turn of events and what a humiliation for Haman! Thinking that *he* was the man the king wanted to honour, he had, himself, provided the king with the "recipe" of the manner in which to honour the man whom the king wished to elevate.

To satisfy his disproportionate ego, he had wanted to have the highest-ranked prince of the kingdom to prepare the cavalcade and to parade him across the city.

And now, tables turned and he had, himself, become the butt of his own joke!

"Mordecai came again to the king's gate. But Haman hurried to his house, mourning and having his head covered.

Haman recounted to Zeresh his wife and all his friends everything that had befallen him. Then said his wise men and Zeresh his wife to him, If Mordecai, before whom you have begun to fall, be of the seed of the Jews, you shall not prevail against him, but shall surely fall before him." [66]

---

[66] Esther 6 :12-13.

Once the cavalcade was over, Mordecai returned to the palace's gate, according to his custom. On the other hand, covered with shame, Haman covered his face and hurried home as fast as he could.

He related to Zeresh, his wife, and to his friends the great humiliation he had been put to. Those were the same ones who had ill-advised him with regard to Mordecai.

It would have been interesting to know how the scene played out when he got back home! How he must have exploded!

My late maternal grandmother used to quote the French proverb '*Les conseilleurs ne sont pas [toujours] les payeurs*".[67]

That was exactly what happened to Haman. He had gullibly followed the advice given by his wife and his friends and he was now the only one to suffer the consequences!

To add insult to injury, his malevolent advisers told him that, if Mordecai before whom he had begun to fall was a Jew, he would never triumph over him: instead, he would go further down!

---

[67] Those who give advice are not always those who pay for the bad consequences thereof.

That looked very much like a prophecy – a word of knowledge! Indeed, the Almighty told Abraham, the father of the Jewish nation, that He would bless all those who would bless Israel and curse all those who would curse her.[68] Moreover, He has already prophesied what will be the end of those who fight against Israel.

"This will be the plague with which Yahweh will strike all the peoples who have warred against Jerusalem: their flesh will consume away while they stand on their feet, and their eyes will consume away in their sockets, and

---

[68] Genesis 12 :2-3.

their tongue will consume away in their mouth."[69]

HAMAN GOES TO THE QUEEN'S BANQUET

"While they were yet talking with him, came the king's chamberlains, and hurried to bring Haman to the banquet that Esther had prepared."[70]

We said above that God has a formidable sense of humour. Let's add that He also has a perfect control over time management. Indeed, being an eternal God, existing in

---

[69] Zechariah 14:12.
[70] Esther 6:14.

timelessness, and having, Himself, created time, He juggles with time at will.

The reason we are saying this here is that, at that very moment, He sends the king's chamberlains to take Haman to the queen's banquet organized in his honour and that of the king.

That was not the first royal banquet Haman had been invited to. Never before did we see anybody coming to fetch him and lead him to the banquet hall!

Fishy, wasn't it?

But Haman must have been blinded by his ego and thought it an additional honour to be led to the banquet by the king's chamberlains.

Let's move on to the next chapter to see how the banquet went on.

End of Act 9.

CHAPTER 15

HAMAN IS HANGED

We may wonder whether the cunning Haman was not suspecting something on his way to the queen's banquet. The great humiliation to which the king, himself, had subjected him ought to have signaled a red flag.

Anyway, even if he had suspected something, his hunch would have been a far guess! Let's see how.

"So the king and Haman came to banquet with Esther the queen.

The king said again to Esther on the second day at the banquet of wine, What is your petition, queen Esther? and it shall be granted you: and what is your request? even to the half of the kingdom it shall be performed.

Then Esther the queen answered, If I have found favor in your sight, O king, and if it please the king, let my life be given me at my petition, and my people at my request:

for we are sold, I and my people, to be destroyed, to be slain, and to perish. But if we had been sold for bondservants and bondmaids, I had held my peace, although the adversary could not have compensated for the king's damage."[71]

On the second day of the banquet, the king must have been again in a state of drunkenness. Notice it was a banquet "of wine"!

Addressing his wife by her formal title, "Queen Esther", the king asked her what her request was. Again, he repeated that, even if it was half of his kingdom, he would grant it.

Now came the moment Esther had long been waiting for! It was time to turn the table over her people's enemy!

---

[71] Esther 7:1-4.

For her, the vengeance dish had grown cold enough to be savoured!

In most respectful terms, she told the king that, if she had found his favour, she implored him to spare her life and the lives of her countrymen for they had been handed over to be massacred – annihilated, even!

She added that, if they had but been sold into slavery, she would have kept quiet although their enemy would not have been able to satisfactorily compensate the king.

Imagine the king's anger when he heard that somebody was planning to kill his wife - the queen - and her people!

"Then spoke the king Ahasuerus and said to Esther the queen, Who is he, and where is he, that dared presume in his heart to do so?

Esther said, An adversary and an enemy, even this wicked Haman. Then Haman was afraid before the king and the queen.

The king arose in his wrath from the banquet of wine [and went] into the palace garden: and Haman stood up to make request for his life to Esther the queen; for he saw that there was evil determined against him by the king."[72]

Mad with anger – an anger exacerbated by his drunkenness – the king asked who was that enemy and where was the one who was

---

[72] Esther 7:5-7.

secretly planning to exterminate the queen and her people.

The king's own words were particularly harsh and fully expressed his fury: *"Who is he, and where is he, that **dared presume in his heart** to do so?"* (emphasis added).

What the king implied was that the culprit – whoever he was - must have been overly audacious to even think he could do what he had been secretly concocting in his mind!

Seeing that the time was opportune, Esther must have said to herself: "It's now or never!"

She told the king that the enemy was nobody else but *"this* Haman"! Saying this, she must have pointed an accusatory finger at Haman.

The latter, quite naturally, got the fright of his life! The king's tone had augured nothing good for him!

Hearing the queen's accusation, the king must have been as furious as Haman was frightened! Who would have thought that the very man he had elevated to such high honour had been planning the extermination of his dear wife and her countrymen? And *there* was that man hypocritically seated at the queen's table, eating *her* food and drinking *her* wine! A real serpent in their midst!

The king must have been shaken by the queen's revelation. He must also have been in a terrible fix, torn between his wife and his favourite.

In order to fully digest what he had just heard and decide upon a course of action, the king left the banquet hall and went to take a walk in the palace garden.

"Then the king returned out of the palace garden into the place of the banquet of wine; and Haman was fallen on the couch whereon Esther was. Then said the king, Will he even force the queen before me in the house? As the word went out of the king's mouth, they covered Haman's face.

Then said Harbonah, one of the chamberlains who were before the king, Behold also, the gallows fifty cubits high, which Haman has made for Mordecai, who spoke good for the king, stands in the house of Haman. The king said, Hang him thereon.

So they hanged Haman on the gallows that he had prepared for Mordecai. Then was the king's wrath pacified."[73]

While the king was taking a stroll in the garden, musing over Haman's treachery, the latter had thrown himself over the couch on which the queen was lying. He was pleading to her to secure the king's pardon.

There's a proverb that says "It never rains but pours" – that is, troubles never come one by one, but in series.

That is what happened to Haman.

---

[73] Esther 7 :8-10.

Indeed, just then, the king came back from the garden and saw him almost lying over the queen. Maybe he was pulling at the queen's robe in his attempt to implore her mercy.

His anger kindled even more, the king thought that Haman was aggressing the queen.

Just then, Harbonah, one of the king's chamberlains, informed the king that the gallows that Haman had prepared for Mordecai was ready.

The king unceremoniously ordered that Haman be hanged thereon and his order was promptly executed.

As we said above, God has a great sense of humour. There, was the wicked Haman "favoured by misfortune" – are we tempted to say - hanged on the very gallows he had prepared for his enemy. What an irony!

When God made a covenant with Abram, He promised to bless those who would bless him and to curse those who would curse him.

In *Esther*, although He is not mentioned by name nor is He personally present, He was, nevertheless, watching over His children to protect them.

The fate that befell Haman was nobody else's doing but His alone!

End of Act 10.

CHAPTER 16

MORDECAI'S RISE TO POWER

Now that Haman has been executed, the whole story takes a completely new turn. The wicked man having undergone a drastic fall from his pedestal, we are now going to see the good Mordecai's rise to power.

From now on, we are going to see a situation diametrically opposite to what we've been seeing so far. A real mirror image!!

"On that day did the king Ahasuerus give the house of Haman the Jews' enemy to Esther the queen. Mordecai came before the king; for Esther had told what he was to her. The king took off his ring, which he had taken from Haman, and gave it to Mordecai. Esther set Mordecai over the house of Haman.

Esther spoke yet again before the king, and fell down at his feet, and begged him with tears to put away the mischief of Haman the Agagite, and his device that he had devised against the Jews." [74]

To begin with, the king confiscated Haman's house and gave it to Esther. Being given the high status Haman had achieved, his house

---

[74] Esther 8: 1-3.

must have been a very large and luxurious one.

Meanwhile, Esther had informed the king of the relationship between her and Mordecai. While the latter had, so far, not been allowed into the palace and had never ventured beyond the gate, now he was introduced personally to the king and could, thus, come into the king's presence.

Esther, in turn and out of gratitude for her dear guardian, gave Mordecai stewardship over Haman's house which was, now, hers.

Quite naturally, the king had taken back his signet ring. He now gave it to Mordecai.

That, alone, was a major honour for Mordecai. As we have already said, the king's signet ring was a token of his sovereignty. Having its custody conferred to the individual absolute authority. We've seen how Haman could use it at will. But he put it to an evil use.

Now that it's Mordecai who had custody of that ring, we can imagine the amount of trust the king had placed in him and the power he now wielded!

As for Esther, seeing that the wind was now blowing in their favour, she fell at the king's feet. With tears flowing down her cheeks, she begged the king to repeal Haman's devilish decree.

Seeing in what sad plight the queen was, the king held out his scepter to her, signifying, by that, that her plea would be favourably entertained.

"Then the king held out to Esther the golden scepter. So Esther arose, and stood before the king.

She said, If it please the king, and if I have found favor in his sight, and the thing seem right before the king, and I be pleasing in his eyes, let it be written to reverse the letters devised by Haman, the son of Hammedatha the Agagite, which he wrote to destroy the Jews who are in all the king's provinces:

for how can I endure to see the evil that shall come to my people? or how can I endure to see the destruction of my relatives?"[75]

Standing up, Esther made to the king a very emotional and heart-moving plea. Showing deep reverence for the king, she addressed her plea to him with no lack of precaution:

- If it pleased the king
- If she had found favour before him
- If her request seemed agreeable to him
- If she was found pleasing by the king

would the king, under those conditions, order that another decree be written to revoke the

---

[75] Esther 8:4-6.

one written by the evil Haman and render it null and void?

With each one of the four conditions she enumerated, she gave the king to understand that it was entirely at his absolute discretion to grant her request. One might think she had read Dale Carnegie's book "*How to Win Friends and Influence People*"!

What is amazing in Esther's behaviour is the profound reverence she had for her husband. I say "amazing" because it's hard in this day and age to see a woman address her husband with such reverence in spite of the fact that the Bible says: "*Wives, be subject to your own husbands, as to the Lord.*"[76]

---

[76] Ephesians 5:22.

Not only was Esther Ahasuerus's wife: she was a queen, too! And, as such, she had quite an amount of power and authority vested in her! Yet, we see how humble she showed herself to be while addressing her husband!

Would that certain modern-day wives treat their husbands with more respect than they actually do!

Then Esther told the king that it would not be possible for her to keep quiet while her own life was in jeopardy. Besides, how could she endure seeing the massacre of her people and of her close ones without, at least, trying something to come to their rescue?

"Then the king Ahasuerus said to Esther the queen and to Mordecai the Jew, See, I have

given Esther the house of Haman, and him they have hanged on the gallows, because he laid his hand on the Jews.

Write you also to the Jews, as it pleases you, in the king's name, and seal it with the king's ring; for the writing which is written in the king's name, and sealed with the king's ring, may no man reverse."[77]

Esther's plea, no doubt, touched the king's heart. He reminded Esther and Mordecai that he had had Haman hanged for having dared decree the massacre of the Jews in the kingdom. In addition, he had seized Haman's house and given it to Esther.

---

[77] Esther 8:7-8.

By saying that, the king was showing his goodwill to Esther and Mordecai and that he now had empathy for the Jews.

Accordingly, he invited Esther and Mordecai to write a new decree in his name and sign it with his ring which was now in Mordecai's custody. The purpose of the new decree was to annul Haman's. If the decree bore the king's signature, nobody but the king would be able to revoke it.

"Then were the king's scribes called at that time, in the third month Sivan, on the three and twentieth [day] of it; and it was written according to all that Mordecai commanded to the Jews, and to the satraps, and the governors and princes of the provinces which

are from India to Ethiopia, one hundred twenty-seven provinces, to every province according to the writing of it, and to every people after their language, and to the Jews according to their writing, and according to their language.

He wrote the name of king Ahasuerus, and sealed it with the king's ring, and sent letters by post on horseback, riding on swift steeds that were used in the king's service, bred of the stud:

in which the king granted the Jews who were in every city to gather themselves together, and to stand for their life, to destroy, to kill, and to cause to perish, all the power of the people and province that would assault them, [their] little ones and women, and to take the spoil of them for a prey,

on one day in all the provinces of king Ahasuerus, [namely], on the thirteenth [day] of the twelfth month, which is the month Adar.

A copy of the writing, that the decree should be given out in every province, was published to all the peoples, and that the Jews should be ready against that day to avenge themselves on their enemies.

So the posts who rode on swift steeds that were used in the king's service went out, being hurried and pressed on by the king's *commandment; and the decree was given out in Shushan the palace.*"[78]

Scribes were promptly called and Mordecai dictated to them the text of the decree.

It stipulated that on a specific day – the thirteenth day of Adar, the twelfth month – the king authorized the Jews to rise in order to defend themselves against all those who wanted to kill them. Instead of being massacred as Haman had wanted it, they had full permission from the king to *"destroy, kill and cause to perish"* all their enemies – men, women and children – and even plunder all their possessions.

---

[78] Esther 8:9-14.

Mordecai's decree was written on the twenty-third day of Sivan, the third month and the Jewish uprising would take place on the thirteenth day of the twelfth month. As that was the exact same date that had been determined by the casting of *Pur*[79] before the late Haman, it means that Mordecai's decree was very timely. Another intervention of God!

The decree was signed with the king's ring and copies were made in all the languages spoken across the kingdom. Couriers were rushed to all the provinces to deliver the decree to all those in authority so that they could publicize it. What was even more

---

[79] Casting of lots.

miraculous was that the king, himself, provided the couriers with fast horses and commanded them to hastily take the decree copies to all the one hundred and twenty-seven provinces!

"Mordecai went forth from the presence of the king in royal clothing of blue and white, and with a great crown of gold, and with a robe of fine linen and purple: and the city of Shushan shouted and was glad.

The Jews had light and gladness, and joy and honor.

In every province, and in every city, wherever the king's commandment and his decree came, the Jews had gladness and joy, a feast and a good day. Many from among the peoples of the land became Jews; for the fear of the Jews was fallen on them."[80]

Once the decree had been written, signed and dispatched, what a relief and what a joy for Mordecai and Esther!

Mordecai now left the king's palace, dressed in royal garments and in fine linen and purple. The cherry on the cake, he donned a royal crown! He had become the kingdom's most eminent personality after the royal couple!

---

[80] Esther 8: 15-17.

All over the kingdom, the atmosphere had radically changed. Crying, weeping, lamenting and mourning had given place to joy, laughter, jubilation and rejoicing! A festive atmosphere now reigned!

Many inhabitants of the kingdom converted to Jewry – such was the fear that the Jews now inspired in the people's minds!

End of Act 11.

CHAPTER 17

D-DAY HAS COME!

When Haman was still in power, he had ordered that *Pur* be cast before him to determine the date on which the extermination of the Jews would take place. The date fixed by the casting of lots was the thirteenth day of Adar, the twelfth month.

Now, that date had arrived but things turned out in reverse!

"Now in the twelfth month, which is the month Adar, on the thirteenth day of the same, when the king's commandment and his decree drew near to be put in execution, on the day that the enemies of the Jews hoped to have rule over them, (whereas it was turned to the contrary, that the Jews had rule over those who hated them,)

the Jews gathered themselves together in their cities throughout all the provinces of the king Ahasuerus, to lay hand on such as sought their hurt: and no man could withstand them; for the fear of them was fallen on all the peoples.

All the princes of the provinces, and the satraps, and the governors, and those who did the king's business, helped the Jews; because the fear of Mordecai was fallen on them.

For Mordecai was great in the king's house, and his fame went forth throughout all the provinces; for the man Mordecai grew greater and greater."[81]

The Jews, therefore, assembled together in the provinces and got ready to execute the provisions of the new decree signed by Mordecai in the king's name.

---

[81] Esther 9:1-4.

When the signal was given for the counterattack to get underway, they all rose and fell upon their enemies, causing a real carnage.

What was even more amazing was that the satraps, governors and other officials in the king's service helped the Jews against their enemies for they feared Mordecai. Not only he now wielded tremendous power, but his power was constantly increasing!

"The Jews struck all their enemies with the stroke of the sword, and with slaughter and destruction, and did what they would to those who hated them.

In Shushan the palace the Jews killed and destroyed five hundred men.

Parshandatha, and Dalphon, and Aspatha,

and Poratha, and Adalia, and Aridatha,

and Parmashta, and Arisai, and Aridai, and Vaizatha,

the ten sons of Haman the son of Hammedatha, the Jew's enemy, killed they; but they didn't lay their hand on the spoil.

On that day the number of those who were slain in Shushan the palace was brought before the king."[82]

Unreservedly supported by the king's decree, the Jews struck with the sword all those who had thought they'd reign over them with

---

[82] Esther 9:5-11.

Haman's blessing. They treated their enemies as they pleased.

In Shushan, the capital, five hundred people were killed and a report was accordingly made to the king.

Among those killed were Haman's ten sons: Parshandatha, Dalphon, Aspatha, Poratha,

Adalia, Aridatha, Parmashta, Arisai, Aridai, and Vaizatha.

How sad for these ten young men who got killed because of their father's wickedness! It's quite possible they were anti-Semitic, too. But, the main source of the problem was their father.

No wonder God says in His Word: "*You shall not bow yourself down to them, nor serve them, for **I, Yahweh your God, am a jealous God, visiting the iniquity of the fathers on the children, on the third and on the fourth generation of those who hate me,***

and showing lovingkindness to thousands of those who love me and keep my commandments."[83]

However, although they were permitted to do so by the decree, the Jews didn't touch any of the possessions of Haman's sons. They must

---

[83] Exodus 20:5-6, emphasis added.

have considered their possessions to be anathema – that is, accursed.[84]

"The king said to Esther the queen, The Jews have slain and destroyed five hundred men in Shushan the palace, and the ten sons of Haman; what then have they done in the rest of the king's provinces! Now what is your petition? and it shall be granted you: or what is your request further? and it shall be done.

Then said Esther, If it please the king, let it be granted to the Jews who are in Shushan to do tomorrow also according to this day's

---

[84] See 1 Samuel 15 for examples.

decree, and let Haman's ten sons be hanged on the gallows.

The king commanded it so to be done: and a decree was given out in Shushan; and they hanged Haman's ten sons.

The Jews who were in Shushan gathered themselves together on the fourteenth day also of the month Adar, and killed three hundred men in Shushan; but they didn't lay their hand on the spoil."[85]

Taking stock of the situation, the king told Esther that if, in Shushan palace only, no fewer than five hundred people had been

_____

[85] Esther 9:12-15.

killed, how many more might have been killed in all the provinces!

Once more, he asked Esther what other petition she had to make. Whatever she might wish to ask, he was prepared to grant her requests!

Jumping on the opportunity, Esther asked the king to allow the Jews in Shushan to continue the killing of their enemies on the next day, the fourteenth day of Adar.

Additionally, she requested that Haman's ten sons be hanged on the gallows – just like their father had been.

Without any surprise, the king granted both of her requests. He sent out another decree for the execution of his wife's desires. Haman's sons' dead bodies were, thus, hanged on the gallows and the massacre of the Jews' enemies went on on the following day in Shushan. Three hundred men were killed but the Jews touched none of their possessions although they were authorized to do so according to the decree.

"The other Jews who were in the king's provinces gathered themselves together, and stood for their lives, and had rest from their enemies, and killed of those who hated them seventy-five thousand; but they didn't lay their hand on the spoil.

[This was done] on the thirteenth day of the month Adar; and on the fourteenth day of the

same they rested, and made it a day of feasting and gladness.

But the Jews who were in Shushan assembled together on the thirteenth [day] of it, and on the fourteenth of it; and on the fifteenth [day] of the same they rested, and made it a day of feasting and gladness.

Therefore do the Jews of the villages, who dwell in the unwalled towns, make the fourteenth day of the month Adar [a day of] gladness and feasting, and a good day, and of sending portions one to another."[86]

---

[86] Esther 9:16-19.

In all the provinces of the kingdom, the killing went on. Seventy-five thousand people were killed but the Jews didn't touch any of their possessions. By the end of the thirteenth day of Adar, the job was done and, thus, the Jews could, at last, enjoy peace.

On the next day, the fourteenth, they rested and feasted to celebrate their liberation.

However, in Shushan – following Esther's request – the carnage went on. On the fifteenth day of Adar, they rested, feasted and jubilated to mark their victory over their enemies.

During the celebration, the Jews exchanged portions of meat among themselves. That was a way of demonstrating their spirit of friendship and unity by bonding them together.

The different days for the massacre and the celebration of victory were to have long term consequences as we shall see in a later chapter.

"Mordecai wrote these things, and sent letters to all the Jews who were in all the provinces of the king Ahasuerus, both near and far,

to enjoin those who they should keep the fourteenth day of the month Adar, and the fifteenth day of the same, yearly, as the days in which the Jews had rest from their enemies, and the month which was turned to them from sorrow to gladness, and from mourning into a good day; that they should make them days of feasting and gladness, and of sending portions one to another, and gifts to the needy.

The Jews undertook to do as they had begun, and as Mordecai had written to them;

because Haman the son of Hammedatha, the Agagite, the enemy of all the Jews, had plotted against the Jews to destroy them, and had cast Pur, that is the lot, to consume them, and to destroy them;

but when [the matter] came before the king, he commanded by letters that his wicked device, which he had devised against the Jews, should return on his own head, and that he and his sons should be hanged on the gallows."[87]

Mordecai had now become the virtual ruler of the kingdom. Having the king's signet ring in his possession and having received *"carte blanche"*[88] from the king, he wrote letters and sent them to all the provinces. In these letters, he enjoined all the Jews to observe that day of celebration as commanded by the king. That day marked a great and miraculous deliverance from their enemies. On that day,

---

[87] Esther 9:20-25.
[88] Full freedom to act as it pleases him.

they ought to have been massacred because of Haman's decree. But the king thwarted his evil plan by writing another decree to order, instead, the massacre of their enemies.

"Therefore they called these days Purim, after the name of Pur. Therefore because of all the words of this letter, and of that which they had seen concerning this matter, and that which had come to them,

the Jews ordained, and took on them, and on their seed, and on all such as joined themselves to them, so that it should not fail, that they would keep these two days according to the writing of it, and according to the appointed time of it, every year;

and that these days should be remembered and kept throughout every generation, every family, every province, and every city; and that these days of Purim should not fail from among the Jews, nor the memory of them perish from their seed."[89]

In all the provinces of the kingdom, the Jews vowed to observe the days of celebration. Those who had become Jews for fear of Mordecai also promised to participate in the celebration. These days came to be known as *Purim* because the date for the massacre of the Jews, originally decided by Haman, had been determined by the casting of *Pur*.

---

[89] Esther 9:26-28.

The matter was of such paramount importance to them that they vowed that they and their descendants, throughout the generations, would observe these days of celebration.

"Then Esther the queen, the daughter of Abihail, and Mordecai the Jew, wrote with all authority to confirm this second letter of Purim.

He sent letters to all the Jews, to the hundred twenty-seven provinces of the kingdom of Ahasuerus, [with] words of peace and truth,

to confirm these days of Purim in their appointed times, according as Mordecai the Jew and Esther the queen had enjoined them, and as they had ordained for themselves and for their seed, in the matter of the fastings and their cry.

The commandment of Esther confirmed these matters of Purim; and it was written in the book."[90]

By now, Mordecai and Esther had become all-powerful. They wrote "with all authority" letters that they sent to all the provinces to enforce the commandment regarding the observance of *Purim*. The letters were written with a spirit of peace and love and insisted

---

[90] Esther 9:29-32.

upon the precise dates on which the celebration was to be observed.

End of Act 12.

CHAPTER 18

GOD'S ROLE IN ESTHER

R ight from the beginning, we said that a major characteristic of the book of ESTHER is that God is never explicitly mentioned in it. However, when we study the story in detail – as we have done in this book – we are bound to recognize that the Almighty is fully at work in the story.

Let's not forget that He says in His Word:

"We know that all things work together for good for those who love God, to those who are called according to his purpose."[91]

God is sovereign. He is Almighty. He is omniscient, omnipotent, omnipresent. As such, He can use any circumstance and turn it to His advantage and to that of those He loves.

We see much of this in Esther.

To begin with, what explains the apparently absurd decision of Mordecai to remain in Persia while he had been given the authorization to return to Jerusalem?

---

[91] Romans 8: 28.

His decision had a direct impact on Esther for, being an orphan and having Mordecai as next of kin, she had to remain in Persia, too. And, as we have seen, God needed Esther in the Persian Empire for a noble purpose. It was He who prompted Mordecai to say these powerful words to Esther:

"For if you altogether hold your peace at this time, then will relief and deliverance arise to the Jews from another place, but you and your father's house will perish: and who knows whether you haven't come to the kingdom for such a time as this?"[92]

---

[92] Esther 4: 14.

The next intervention of God had to do with Vashti. He used the feast during which Ahasuerus was in a state of drunkenness and decided to send for Vashti.

If God needed a Jewish queen in the kingdom of Persia for His purpose, Vashti had to be got rid of, as it were. But how to bring that about? Vashti refused to obey the king's command and was banished.

We have said and seen that the king was surrounded by ambitious and self-seeking counsellors. Is it possible that God used them for His purpose? Does God ever use evil people for His purpose?

*"The LORD has made everything for its own purpose, **Even the wicked** [according to their role] for the day of evil."*[93]

Yes, God is Sovereign and can use anyone and anything to carry out His purpose!

He used the king's counsellors to advise the king to banish Vashti and have a new queen chosen among the kingdom's most beautiful virgins.

Granted Esther was beautiful and virgin. So it's natural that she found herself among the young maidens taken to the women's house on the palace compound.

---

[93] Proverbs 16:4, Amplified Bible. Emphasis added.

But how can we explain the favour she received from the eunuch in charge of the maidens? She was given a VIP treatment, as it were, and was even moved to a special apartment!

Better still, what explains that, when she went to the king, he found that she pleased him much more than the others? As we said in a previous chapter, was she the last maiden to spend the night with the king so he could make an appraisal of them all and conclude that Esther was the one who pleased him the most?

The probability was very small! What special treatment could she have given the king that caused him to crown her queen? Was it just *her* doing or was the Almighty at work behind the scene?

Now that Esther had been established queen, she was enjoying the wealth, the luxury, the pomp and all the prestige associated with her condition. Living within the safety and the security of the palace, she was not aware of what was going on outside the palace.

That's when God used Mordecai to keep a communication line with the queen. It was via the faithful Mordecai that Esther would know that her countrymen – and maybe herself - were under a terrible threat of annihilation. And, as Mordecai told her, her own relatives and herself might not be spared in the genocide! We have described Mordecai's key role in chapter 11.

As we said above, God has even created wicked people for His purpose.

Haman fell in this category. God used him very much like He used the Pharaoh in Egypt to demonstrate His Supremacy. He broke the Pharaoh's pride, cast him down and set His children free. Similarly, He dealt with Haman. He brought Haman down from his pedestal. The latter was hanged and Mordecai was honoured!

God's intervention is also seen through all the favours Esther received from the king. Each time she appeared before the king, it was *he* who asked her what petition she had to make and not once did the king refuse to grant her whatever she asked. On several occasions, he was even prepared to give her half of His kingdom!

Haman's execution on the very gallows he had prepared for Mordecai, the reversal of his decree in favour of the Jews and the massacre of the enemies of the Jews on the very date determined by lots cast before Haman had all to be by Divine intervention!

In short, a careful study of ESTHER proves without any contest that God, the Great Director, was at work behind the stage to bring His Plan to fruition – His Plan being to rescue His children from annihilation!

As He said to Abraham, the father of the Jewish nation, *"I will bless those who bless you and curse those who curse you."*[94]

---

[94] Genesis 12:3.

CHAPTER 19

THE TRINITY IN ESTHER

Now that we have come to the end of the study of ESTHER, we have had the conviction that nowhere and not once in the book is God specifically mentioned.

But, as we have said a number of times, He is, nevertheless, present and active in the story. Indeed, the story is full of coincidences. When coincidences become too numerous, we are bound to stop calling them "coincidences": it's time we call that "Plan"!

Yes, the story of Esther exposes a wonderful Plan of God – one of the most beautiful ones in the whole Bible!

If we speak of a Plan, there *has* to be a purpose to it. the purpose behind God's Plan in ESTHER was the salvation of His people from an evil plan of destruction.

Far from us the idea of glorifying the devil. But the apostle Paul gives us a very severe and urgent warning regarding him:

"Put on the whole armor of God, that you may be able to stand against the wiles of the devil.

For our wrestling is not against flesh and blood, but against the principalities, against the powers, against the world's rulers of the darkness of this age, and against the spiritual hosts of wickedness in the heavenly places."[95]

If we are commanded to put on "t*he whole armor*" of God, it means that the battle is going to be tough!

Indeed, the devil's army, as the Scriptures above define it, is a very well organized one. There is a real hierarchy within it with the devil at the head of it.

---

[95] Ephesians 6:11-12.

What I mean is that, in ESTHER, the devil had a well-organized plan to destroy the Jews, God's people. It was systematic, scientific, clinical!

To counter-attack and thwart his plan, there had to be a yet better plan. Just like God had a much better Plan to destroy the Pharaoh's plan against the Israelites in Egypt.

God, therefore, came forward with a Master Plan. He put it in action in a way only *He* could have imagined!

He used the exact strategy the enemy had planned to use and used it against the main instigator and his cohorts!

To write God's inspired Word, the human authors used a lot of imagery and figurative language – such as in *Ezekiel*, *Daniel* and *Revelation*, the main eschatological books.

The Book of Esther is no exception to the rule. It is full of symbolisms. These are mostly in connection with the main characters.

Of course, we must guard ourselves against over-spiritualizing. But the fact remains that certain symbolisms are all too obvious.

Let's look at some of them.

The most obvious one is, unquestionably, Haman. He is an exact picture of the devil.

Ever since Lucifer rebelled against God in Heaven and was cast down to earth, he's been mad with anger.

"Woe for the earth and for the sea, because the devil has gone down to you, having great wrath, knowing that he has but a short time."[96]

Defeated, debarred and dethroned by God, he began launching his evil attacks against God's creation. It all started with Adam and Eve who, unfortunately, allowed themselves to be deceived.

After God called Abram (Abraham) and made an alliance with him and his seed, the battle became more ferocious. The period

---

[96] Revelation 12:12.

during which the Israelites were in slavery in Egypt is by far the best description of how the devil used a man and a people – Pharaoh and the Egyptians - to exploit and crush God's chosen people.

In modern times, the harshest period of persecution against the Jews was definitely the Holocaust during World War II. Never before nor since has a people been treated so inhumanely!

Now that we are in the end times, anti-Semitism – hatred of the Jews – is spreading almost all over the world. Recently, against the backdrop of the war in Gaza, we have seen how in the U.S – once a Christian country – there have been wild anti-Jewish demonstrations. Even University campuses were invaded and occupied by anti-Jewish – pro-Palestinian demonstrators!

God, in His omniscience, has prophesied that this anti-Jewish sentiment will rise crescendo to culminate in the Battle of Armageddon when Jesus will crush that mega-rebellion and establish His Eternal Kingdom.

In ESTHER, we see the Jewish people in danger of being massacred by a devil's pawn called Haman.

To come to the rescue of His people, God used Esther, a symbol of the Gentile Church.

Indeed, Hadassah, the Myrtle, was in exile. By a series of miraculous circumstances, God brought her into the king's Court and made her queen. From Hadassah, the Myrtle, she became Esther, the Star.

As her guardian, Mordecai made her realize, there had to be a reason why, against all odds, she had become queen of Persia.

God, in His prescience, wanted her there to intercede for His children. He had foreknown the evil plan that would, one day, be put into place to destroy His people.

In the face of so much hatred growing against the Jewish people, the Gentile Church must now, like Esther, make intercession for the Jewish people.

Remember Jesus said that salvation is of the Jews![97] And for Paul, when we, Gentiles, become Christians, we are like wild olives grafted on the true olive[98] – Israel. In other words, just like the grafted wild olives benefit from the sap of the true olive, so do we benefit from the blessings of Israel, the Chosen People of God.

Another interesting – and, by far the most important – character in ESTHER is, as we have seen, Mordecai.

He is Esther's guardian, he is constantly found near the king's palace, he is deeply and affectionately concerned about her welfare,

---

[97] John 4:22.
[98] Romans 11:17.

he informs Esther of the plot against the king's life, he is the one who writes the second edict to revoke that written by Haman and he ends up becoming the kingdom's highest ranking official after the royal couple.

His role can, to a certain degree, be likened to that of the Holy Spirit. Just as Jesus has given us the Holy Spirit to watch over the Church, to guide her in all the truth and to teach her everything, so does Mordecai watch over Esther – a symbol of the Church – informs and instructs her.

What about king Ahasuerus? Some commentators associate him with God the Father.

But I, personally, find him to be more like Jesus – at least, in the role he plays.

Of course, we cannot stretch these parallels too far. As we said, we must guard against over-spiritualizing. For example, it would be blasphemous to view Jesus as addicted to wine as Ahasuerus. Or, as a monarch with a whole harem at his disposal!

The association between Ahasuerus and Jesus lies, rather, in the area of the headship. Just as Jesus is the Head of the Church, so is Ahasuerus, the husband, the head of Esther, the wife.[99]

Another common point between Ahasuerus and Jesus is in the area of intercession. Just as

---

[99] Ephesians 5:23.

the Church addresses her petitions to Jesus, who is the way to the Father, so does Esther plead to Ahasuerus for protection over the Church.

But then, who is God the Father? I believe He is not represented by any specific character in the story. But, as I have already said, He is like a film Director in so far as He guides, instructs, supervises, oversees and controls the set but is not personally present on the stage. From behind the stage, He sees to it that the scenario is well adhered to.

As the apostle Paul puts it, *"We know that all things work together for good for those who love God, to those who are called according to his purpose."*[100]

The story of Esther is a perfect illustration of that.

---

[100] Romans 8:28.

CHAPTER 20

THE FESTIVAL OF PURIM

The festival of Purim has become one of the most important ones in the Jewish calendar. It finds its origin in the story of Esther.

The word "*Purim*" is the plural of the word "*Pur*" and means "lots".

As we have seen, Ahasuerus's officials cast lots before Haman to determine a date for the extermination of the Jews and the date chosen

241

was the thirteenth day of Adar, the twelfth month of the year.[101] Adar generally falls in February-March.

The ritual begins on the 13th of Adar with a day of fasting called *"Ta'anit Esther"* – the fast of Esther.[102] "Purim" is celebrated on two different dates: the 13th-14th days of Adar in unwalled cities like Tel Aviv and the 14th-15th days of Adar in Jerusalem, a walled city.

This is because it was first celebrated on the 13th-14th of Adar. Then, at Esther's request, it was prolonged in Shushan, the walled

---

[101] Esther 9:26-28.
[102] Britannica, The Editors of Encyclopaedia. "Lag ba-'Omer". Encyclopedia Britannica, 11 Jul. 2024, https://www.britannica.com/topic/Lag-ba-Omer. Accessed 29 July 2024.

capital of the Persian Empire, on the 14th-15th of Adar.

Purim is a festival of joy – in fact, the most joyous festival of the Jewish calendar. Indeed, it commemorates the liberation of the Jews at the hands of the wicked Haman.

There are a number of traditions and practices associated with the festival.

The celebration begins in the synagogue with the reading of the *Megillah*,[103] that is the scroll containing the story of Esther. This is also referred to *"M'gillat Esther"*[104].

---

[103] Chabad.org: http://chabad.org>...The Megillah. Accessed 29 July 2024.
[104] Reform Judaism.org. http://reformjudaism.org>purim-customs-and-rituals. Purim Customs and Rituals. Accessed 29 July 2024.

During the reading, each time the name "Haman" is mentioned, it is accompanied by loud boos, foot stamping and noises made by groggers.[105] This is done to express contempt and hatred for Haman.

It is customary to send gifts and food to friends and relatives as a sign of camaraderie. This exchange of gifts is called *Mishloach Manot*.[106]

Gifts and food are given to the poor according to a custom called *"matanot l'evyonim"*.[107]

---

[105] Chabad.org: http://chabad.org>...The Megillah. Accessed 29 July 2024.

[106] https://marom.org>purim-the-story-behind Purim Traditions: The Story Behind the Celebration-Marom. Accessed 29 July 2024.

[107] Chabad.org: http://chabad.org>...The Megillah. Accessed 29 July 2024.

The aim is for everybody to have enough to celebrate the festival.

A special meal called *"Seudah"*[108] is served to strengthen the family bond. At table, a special triangular-shaped cake is served called *"Hamantaschen"*.[109] These are three-cornered cakes with poppy seeds, chocolate or fruit preserve fillings. Their bizarre shape is a mockery of Haman's ears or of his hat which, it is believed, had that shape.

---

[108] "Seudah." Merriam-Webster.com Dictionary, Merriam-Webster, https://www.merriam-webster.com/dictionary/seudah. Accessed 30 Jul. 2024.
[109] Chabad.org: http://chabad.org>...The **Megillah**. Accessed 29 July 2024.

As Purim is a festival of joy, they also perform humorous plays called *"Purim spiels"*[110] – also spelt *"shpiels"*.

In Tel Aviv, especially, the celebration is even more joyous and festive. People parade in the streets, disguised as certain characters of the Book of Esther or as other Jewish heroes.

We have seen how wine drinking plays an important role in the story. During the festival, some drink so much that they can't tell right from wrong![111]

---

[110] Chabad.org: http://chabad.org>...The Megillah. Accessed 29 July 2024.
[111] Judaica Web Store. http://blog.judaicawebstore> Purim Traditions Explained. Accessed 29 July 20224.

In short, "Purim" is a joyous festival that commemorates the miraculous liberation of the Jews from utter destruction. It also demonstrates their resilience in spite of cruel persecution.

Last but not least, Purim is a reminder of God's resolution to protect and save His chosen People no matter what the situation may be.

CHAPTER 21

CONCLUSION

As we have already said, ESTHER is one of the only two books in the Bible that bear women's names. The other one is RUTH.

We have also said that the true author of the book is not known: there are only speculations regarding its authorship.

ESTHER is a very unusual book in so far as God is not even once explicitly mentioned in it.

For that reason, its inclusion in the canon of Scripture has been a matter of debate.

It is also a book in which the story takes place entirely in a foreign country. Although it's all about the Jewish people, it is, nevertheless, based entirely in Persia.

It's true that God is never mentioned in the book. But, as we have amply explained, He is very active, acting through people and circumstances.

Although some of the characters – especially Ahasuerus, Esther and Mordecai – can, to a certain degree, be likened to certain Persons of the Trinity and the Church, we see, however, that those characters do not fully uphold "Christian" and "Biblical" principles.

The story, itself, is set in a pagan country and, more specifically, in a palace where wine, sexual pleasure, polygamy, nepotism, hatred, jealousy, ambition, treachery, death and other forms of immorality prevail and abound!

It's hard also to understand Ahasuerus's character.

Indeed, we are at a loss to understand how such a great and powerful monarch who was at the head of such a vast kingdom could have been so weak and fickle-minded! How can we explain that he relied that much on advisers even in matters concerning his conjugal life? How can we explain that he so lacked perspicacity as to not foresee where their ill-inspired advice would lead him?

How can we understand that he so readily surrendered his authority to others by giving them his signet ring? Finally, how could he so often and so "unsolicitedly" offer half of his kingdom to his wife? Was it because he was under the power of love or rather under the power of wine?

Had Esther accepted his offer each time he came forward with it, he would, in the end, have found himself with no kingdom at all: all of it would have become Esther's property!

It seems that he was much more interested in indulging in carousing, drinking and debauchery than in administering the affairs of the country!

In short, Ahasuerus quite strangely proved to be a very weak monarch. He seems to have been more a caricature than a potentate!

That's why, in disagreement with some commentators, I refuse to liken him to God the Father.

Nevertheless, the fact remains that ESTHER is one of the most mysterious, most beautiful and most inspiring books of the Bible.

To my mind, the real beauty of the book lies precisely in the fact that God is not a single time mentioned in it.

Yet, His Love, His Compassion, His Wisdom, and His Power to save His People are all visible and active in this marvellous book.

Its inclusion in the canon of Scripture is, to my mind, fully justified and warranted.